Generative AI for

I0008275

Innovate Faster - Build Next-Gen Applications with AI-Generated Code

Sergio Robert

Table of Contents

Preface

Hey there, fellow coders! If you're picking up this book, you're probably just as excited as I am about what's happening in the world of AI, specifically how it's changing the way we build software. Honestly, it feels like we're standing at the edge of something incredible. For years, we've been crafting code line by line, solving problems with logic and persistence. Now, we're starting to see AI step in, not to replace us, but to partner with us, to amplify our abilities. Imagine having a collaborator that can generate code snippets, automate tedious tasks, and even spark new ideas. That's what this book is about—making that partnership a reality.

Background and Motivation

The idea for this book came from my own experience exploring generative AI. Like many of you, I was both fascinated and a little overwhelmed by the rapid advancements. I saw the potential to revolutionize how we code, but finding practical, developer-focused resources was a challenge. I wanted to create something that cut through the jargon, something that showed real, actionable ways to use these tools. I wanted to share the excitement of seeing AI generate code that actually works, and the satisfaction of building smarter applications faster. I believe we are entering a new phase of software development, and I want to help us all get there.

Purpose and Scope

This book aims to be your practical guide to incorporating generative AI into your coding toolkit. We're going to explore how to use AI models to generate code, automate tasks, and build next-generation applications. We'll look at the fundamental concepts of generative AI, learn how to set up our development environments, and discuss real-world examples of how to apply these techniques. My goal is to equip you with the knowledge and skills to leverage AI effectively, making you a more efficient and innovative developer.

Target Audience

This book is written for you—the software developers, the problem solvers, the creators. Whether you're a seasoned professional or just starting out, if you're curious about how AI can enhance your coding, you'll find something valuable here. We'll be focusing on practical applications and clear explanations, so you can jump right in and start experimenting.

Organization and Structure

We've organized the book into three main sections. First, we'll build a solid foundation by understanding the core concepts of generative AI and setting up our development environment. Then, we'll move into practical applications, exploring real-world examples of how to use AI to generate code, automate tasks, and build innovative applications. Finally, we'll look at advanced topics, including fine-tuning models, AI-driven software architecture, and the ethical considerations of using AI in development.

Invitation to Read

I'm genuinely excited for you to start exploring the possibilities of generative AI. This isn't just a theoretical exercise; it's about giving you the tools to build the future. So, let's get started. Open this book, follow along with the examples, and let's see what amazing things we can create together. Happy coding!

Chapter 1: The Dawn of AI-Assisted Coding

Alright, let's talk about the future of coding, but before we get there, we need to understand where we've come from. Think about it: coding hasn't always been the way it is now. We started with these massive machines, punch cards, and languages that were practically alien to us. It was a whole different world, right?

1.1 The Evolution of Software Development

Let's talk about how we got here, shall we? You know, the coding world wasn't always as fancy as it is today. It's easy to forget, with all our modern IDEs and frameworks, that it started with something a bit... simpler. Or, well, technically, a lot more complex, but in a different way.

Picture this: the early days of computers. We're talking mainframes, those room-sized machines that hummed and whirred.[1] To interact with them, you used punch cards.[2] Yes, those cardboard cards with holes in them.[3] Each hole represented a piece of data or an instruction.[4] It was a painstaking process, and if you made a mistake, you had to redo the whole card.[5]

Then came assembly language. This was a step up. Instead of punching holes, you could write short, mnemonic codes that represented machine instructions.[6] It was still very low-level, meaning you were close to the hardware, but it was more human-readable than punch cards. Even with assembly, writing complex programs was incredibly time-consuming.[7]

Let's take a look at a simple assembly example. For a hypothetical CPU, adding two numbers might look something like this:

Code snippet

LOAD A, 5 ; Load the value 5 into register A

LOAD B, 10 ; Load the value 10 into register B

ADD A, B ; Add the values in registers A and B, store in A

STORE RESULT, A ; Store the result in memory location RESULT

As you can see, even a basic addition requires several instructions. It's not exactly intuitive, is it?

Then, high-level languages arrived. Languages like FORTRAN, COBOL, and later C. These languages let you write code that was closer to human language. You could write expressions like result = a + b instead of fiddling with registers. This made programming more accessible to a wider audience, and it sped up development significantly.[8]

Think about C for a moment. It's a powerful language that's still used today, especially in systems programming.[9]

A simple "Hello, world!" program in C looks like this:

C

```
#include <stdio.h>


int main() {

    printf("Hello, world!\n");

    return 0;

}
```

This is much easier to understand than assembly, isn't it? We're starting to see code that resembles English.

Object-oriented programming (OOP) took things a step further.[10] Languages like C++, Java, and later Python introduced the concept of objects, which allowed developers to model real-world entities in their code.[11] This made it easier to organize and reuse code, leading to more modular and maintainable applications.

Consider a simple Java class:

Java

```java
public class Car {

    String make;

    String model;


    public Car(String make, String model) {

        this.make = make;

        this.model = model;

    }


    public void displayInfo() {

        System.out.println("Make: " + make + ",
Model: " + model);

    }
```

```
public static void main(String[] args) {

    Car myCar = new Car("Toyota", "Camry");

    myCar.displayInfo();

}

}
```

This code models a "Car" as an object with attributes and methods. This is OOP in action, making code more structured and reusable.

Then, the internet happened. Suddenly, we weren't just writing programs for individual computers anymore. We were building web applications, connecting to databases, and dealing with complex network protocols. This brought about a whole new set of challenges and technologies. We had to learn about HTML, CSS, JavaScript, and various server-side languages.

Think about a simple web page.

HTML lets us structure content:

HTML

```
<!DOCTYPE html>

<html>

<head>

    <title>My Web Page</title>

</head>

<body>

    <h1>Welcome!</h1>
```

```
    <p>This is my first web page.</p>

</body>

</html>
```

And JavaScript lets us add interactivity:

JavaScript

```
document.addEventListener('DOMContentLoaded',
function() {

    let heading = document.querySelector('h1');

    heading.addEventListener('click', function()
{

        alert('You clicked the heading!');

    });

});
```

We now have code that runs in a browser, interacts with users, and communicates with servers.

Today, we have powerful IDEs that provide features like code completion, debugging, and version control.[12] We have frameworks that simplify complex tasks. We have cloud computing platforms that let us deploy applications at scale.[13] But even with all these advancements, the fundamental challenge remains: we still have to translate our ideas into code.

And that's where AI comes in. It's the next step in this evolution, a way to make coding even more efficient and accessible. But we'll get to that. For now, take a moment to appreciate how far we've come. We've gone from punch cards to complex web applications, and each step has built upon the previous one. It's a continuous process, and we're all part of it.

1.2 The Rise of Generative AI

So, we've talked about how coding has changed over the years. Now, let's get into something that's really shaking things up: generative AI. You've probably heard the buzzwords, but what does it actually mean for us, as coders?

Essentially, generative AI is about creating new content using machine learning. It's not just about analyzing data; it's about making something new. This could be anything from images and music to, most importantly for us, code. And it's not some far-off concept; it's happening right now.

Think about language models, for instance. Models like GPT, or specifically for our use, models designed specifically for code generation like Codex or CodeT5. These models are trained on absolutely massive datasets. In the case of code, they've been fed huge amounts of publicly available code, from GitHub and other sources. This allows them to learn the patterns, structures, and even the "style" of different programming languages.

How does this work in practice? Well, these models use something called neural networks, specifically transformer architectures. These networks are designed to understand relationships between words or, in our case, code elements. They learn to predict the next token (a word, a character, or a piece of code) in a sequence based on the tokens that came before.

Let's take a simple example. Suppose we want to generate a Python function that adds two numbers.

We might give the AI a prompt like this:

```python
Python

# Function to add two numbers

def add_numbers(a, b):
```

The AI, having been trained on a vast dataset of Python code, can then predict what comes next.

It might generate something like this:

```python
Python

# Function to add two numbers

def add_numbers(a, b):
    """

    This function takes two numbers as input and
returns their sum.

    """

    return a + b
```

Notice how it not only generates the core logic but also includes a docstring, which is good practice. This is because it has learned from the many examples of well-documented code in its training data.

Now, this is a very simple example. But these models can handle much more complex tasks. They can generate entire functions, classes, and even applications based on natural language descriptions or existing code snippets.

For instance, consider a more complex scenario where we want to generate a function that reads data from a CSV file and performs some data processing. We might give the AI a prompt like this:

```python
Python

# Function to read data from a CSV file and
process it

import pandas as pd


def process_csv(filename):
```

The AI might generate something like this:

```python
Python

# Function to read data from a CSV file and
process it

import pandas as pd


def process_csv(filename):

    """

    Reads data from a CSV file, performs some
data processing, and returns the processed data.

    """

    df = pd.read_csv(filename)

    # Perform some data processing here
```

```
df['processed_data'] = df['column1'] * 2

return df
```

Here, the AI has used the pandas library, which is a common tool for data processing in Python. It has also added a basic data processing step. This shows how it can understand and use external libraries and complex data structures.

It's important to understand that these models aren't just copying and pasting code. They're learning the underlying patterns and structures of code, allowing them to generate new and original code. This is what makes them so powerful.

But how does this help us as coders? Well, it can automate repetitive tasks, generate boilerplate code, and even help us explore new ideas. It's like having a coding partner that can suggest solutions and generate code snippets on demand.

For example, imagine you're working on a web application and need to create a form. Instead of writing all the HTML and JavaScript from scratch, you could use generative AI to generate the code for you. Or, imagine you need to write a unit test for a complex function. You could use AI to generate the test cases and assertions.

This isn't about replacing coders; it's about augmenting our abilities. It's about making us more efficient and allowing us to focus on the more creative and challenging aspects of software development.

Now, you might be thinking, "This sounds too good to be true. Are there any downsides?" And that's a fair question. These models can sometimes generate code that is incorrect or inefficient. They can also perpetuate biases that exist in their training data.

That's why it's crucial to understand how these models work and to use them responsibly. We need to treat them as tools, not as replacements for our own judgment. We need to review and test the generated code carefully.

But even with these limitations, the potential of generative AI for coders is immense. It's a new frontier, and we're just beginning to explore its possibilities. It's an exciting time to be a coder, and I'm looking forward to seeing what we can build together.

1.3 Potential Benefits and Impact

Alright, let's talk about why we should be excited about generative AI in coding. It's not just a cool tech demo; it has the potential to fundamentally change how we build software. We're talking about real, tangible benefits that can make our lives as coders easier and more productive.

First off, think about automation. We spend a lot of time on repetitive tasks, right? Writing boilerplate code, setting up configurations, creating unit tests – these are necessary, but they can be a real time sink. Generative AI can take a lot of that off our plates.

Take, for example, the task of generating API documentation. We have tools that help, but they still require manual input. With generative AI, we could simply provide the API's code and a brief description of its functionality, and the AI could generate comprehensive documentation, including examples and usage instructions.

Consider this Python example:

```
Python

# Our API function

def calculate_area(length, width):
```

```
    """Calculates the area of a rectangle."""

    return length * width


# Prompt for AI: Generate documentation for the
above function.
```

The AI could generate something like this:

Function: calculate_area

Description: Calculates the area of a rectangle.

Parameters:

    length (int): The length of the rectangle.

    width (int): The width of the rectangle.

Returns:

    int: The area of the rectangle.

Example:

    >>> calculate_area(5, 10)

    50

This kind of automation frees us up to focus on the more complex and creative aspects of development. We can spend more time designing architectures, solving challenging problems, and innovating.

Another major benefit is the sheer speed of code generation. Need a function to perform a specific task? You can describe it in natural language, and the AI can generate the code for you. This means we can prototype ideas much faster. We can experiment with different approaches and see results almost instantly.

Let's say you need a function to sort a list of dictionaries based on a specific key.

You could write a prompt like this:

Python

```
# Prompt: Generate a Python function to sort a
list of dictionaries by a given key.
```

The AI might generate something like this:

Python

```
def sort_dictionaries(list_of_dicts, key):

    """Sorts a list of dictionaries by a given
key."""

    return sorted(list_of_dicts, key=lambda x:
x[key])
```

This can significantly reduce the time spent on writing routine code, allowing us to focus on the logic that really matters.

Beyond speed, generative AI can also help us explore new ideas. It can generate code that we might not have thought of, suggesting alternative approaches and solutions. This can spark creativity and lead to more innovative software.

Imagine you're working on a data visualization project. You could ask the AI to generate different chart types based on your data, and it might suggest visualizations that you hadn't considered. This can help you gain new insights and create more compelling visualizations.

Furthermore, AI can help us improve code quality. It can analyze our code and suggest improvements, identify potential bugs, and even generate unit tests. This can lead to more robust and reliable software.

Think of it like having a built-in code reviewer that's always available. The AI can help us catch common errors and enforce coding standards, ensuring that our code is clean and maintainable.

Consider this example where the AI provides a suggestion on a code structure.

Python

```python
# Original code:

def process_data(data):

    results = []

    for item in data:

        if item > 10:

            results.append(item * 2)

        else:

            results.append(item)
```

```
    return results
```

```
# AI suggestion:

# Consider using list comprehensions for more
concise code.
```

The AI could then provide the improved code:

```
Python

def process_data(data):

    return [item * 2 if item > 10 else item for
item in data]
```

This suggestion not only improves readability but also makes the code more efficient.

Finally, generative AI can democratize coding. It can make programming more accessible to beginners, allowing them to build applications without extensive programming knowledge. Imagine someone who has an idea for an app but doesn't know how to code. With AI, they could describe their idea, and the AI could generate the code for them.

This has the potential to open up coding to a whole new audience, fostering innovation and creativity. It could also make coding more accessible to people with disabilities, who might find traditional coding methods challenging.

Of course, there are challenges and limitations. We need to use these tools responsibly and critically evaluate the generated code. But the potential benefits are undeniable. Generative AI is going to change how we develop software, and it's up to us to embrace it and use it to build a better future.

1.4 Demystifying AI for Coders

Let's be honest, the term "artificial intelligence" can sound a little intimidating, right? Especially when we think about applying it directly to our coding practices. It's easy to picture complex algorithms and mathematical equations that seem miles away from our day-to-day work. But here's the thing: we don't need to be AI experts to use these tools effectively. We can approach it like we approach any other technology – as a tool in our toolbox.

Think about it this way: when you use a library or a framework, do you need to understand every single line of code that goes into its creation? Probably not. You use it because it solves a problem and makes your life easier. Generative AI is similar. We're going to treat it as a powerful tool that can help us write code more efficiently and creatively.

So, let's break down some of the common misconceptions and demystify AI for coders.

First off, there's the idea that AI is some kind of magical black box. We input something, and it outputs something else, and we have no idea how it works. That's not entirely true. While the internal workings of large language models can be complex, we can understand the basic principles.

These models are trained on massive datasets, as we discussed. They learn patterns and relationships in the data. In the case of code, they learn the syntax, semantics, and even the style of different programming languages. They use neural networks, specifically transformer architectures, to process and generate code. These networks are designed to understand the context of the code and predict what comes next.

Think of it like learning a new language. You start by learning the basic vocabulary and grammar, and then you gradually build your understanding of the language's structure and nuances. The AI models do something similar, but they do it on a much larger scale and at a much faster pace.

Now, let's look at how we can interact with these models. We're not going to be training them from scratch. Instead, we'll be using pre-trained models through APIs or libraries. This is similar to using any other external service in our code.

For example, many AI code generation services provide APIs that we can use to send prompts and receive generated code.

A simple Python example of interacting with such an API might look like this:

```python
Python

import requests


def generate_code(prompt):

    api_url =
"https://api.example-ai.com/generate_code"

    headers = {"Authorization": "Bearer
YOUR_API_KEY"}

    data = {"prompt": prompt}


    response = requests.post(api_url,
headers=headers, json=data)


    if response.status_code == 200:
```

```
        return response.json()["generated_code"]

    else:

        return "Error: " + response.text


# Example usage

prompt = "# Python function to reverse a string"

generated_code = generate_code(prompt)

print(generated_code)
```

In this example, we're sending a prompt to an AI code generation API and receiving the generated code as a response. We're using the requests library, which is a common tool for making HTTP requests in Python.

We don't need to understand the inner workings of the AI model to use this API. We just need to know how to send a request and process the response.

Another common misconception is that AI-generated code is always perfect. It's not. These models can sometimes generate code that is incorrect, inefficient, or even insecure. That's why it's crucial to review and test the generated code carefully.

Think of it like getting help from a junior developer. You wouldn't just blindly trust their code, right? You would review it, test it, and make sure it meets your standards. The same applies to AI-generated code.

We also need to be aware of the ethical implications of using AI in coding. These models can perpetuate biases that exist in their training data. For example, if the model is trained on code that reflects certain stereotypes, it might generate code that reinforces those stereotypes.

We need to be mindful of these issues and use AI responsibly. We need to critically evaluate the generated code and ensure that it aligns with our values and principles.

Finally, let's talk about the learning curve. Yes, there is a learning curve associated with using generative AI. But it's not as steep as you might think. We're not talking about learning advanced machine learning concepts. We're talking about learning how to write effective prompts, how to use the available tools and APIs, and how to integrate AI-generated code into our workflows.

Think of it like learning a new framework or library. It takes time and effort, but it's worth it in the long run.

In essence, demystifying AI for coders is about making it approachable and understandable. It's about treating it as a tool that can enhance our abilities, not replace them. It's about learning how to use it effectively and responsibly. And it's about being open to the possibilities that it offers.

Chapter 2: Core Concepts of Generative AI

Alright, let's get into the nitty-gritty of how generative AI actually works, especially as it relates to coding. I know, it might sound a bit technical, but we'll break it down into something you can really understand and use. We need to understand the foundations before we can really leverage the power of these tools.

2.1 Neural Networks and Transformers

Let's get down to the brass tacks of what powers a lot of this generative AI magic: neural networks and, more specifically, transformers. Now, I know these terms can sound a bit intimidating, but trust me, they're not as complicated as they seem once we break them down.

First, let's talk about neural networks. At their core, they're computational models designed to mimic how the human brain works. Of course, they're a vastly simplified version, but the underlying principle is the same: processing information through interconnected nodes.

Think of a neural network as a series of layers. Each layer contains nodes, or "neurons," that perform calculations on the input they receive. The output of one layer then becomes the input for the next, and so on, until we reach the final layer, which produces the output.

Each connection between neurons has an associated "weight," which determines how much influence that connection has on the output. These weights are adjusted during the training process, allowing the network to learn patterns and relationships in the data.

Let's illustrate this with a very simplified example. Imagine we have a neural network that predicts whether an email is spam or not. We might feed it features like the number of capital letters, the presence of certain keywords, and the length of the email.

The network would then process these features through its layers, adjusting the weights of the connections to produce a probability of the email being spam. If the probability is above a certain threshold, we classify the email as spam.

Now, traditional neural networks have been around for a while, but they have limitations, especially when it comes to handling sequential data like text or code. This is where transformers come in.

Transformers are a specific type of neural network architecture that has revolutionized the field of natural language processing and, consequently, code generation. What makes them so powerful is their ability to understand context.

Unlike traditional neural networks, which process input sequentially, transformers can process the entire input sequence at once. They use a mechanism called "attention" to weigh the importance of different parts of the input.

This attention mechanism is what allows transformers to understand the relationships between words or code elements, even if they're far apart. For example, when generating code, a transformer can understand that a variable declared at the beginning of a function is still relevant later on.

Let's break down the attention mechanism a bit. Imagine we have a sentence: "The cat chased the mouse because it was fast." To understand what "it" refers to, a transformer would look at all the words in the sentence and assign weights to them, indicating their relevance. In this case, the word "cat" would likely have a higher weight than the word "because."

In code, this translates to understanding the relationships between variables, functions, and classes. A transformer can identify which parts of the code are most relevant to the current task and use that information to generate new code.

Here's a simplified conceptual example of how a transformer might process a code snippet:

Python

```python
# Original code:

def calculate_average(numbers):

    total = 0

    for number in numbers:

        total += number

    return total / len(numbers)

# Conceptual transformer process:

# The transformer would analyze the code and
assign weights to different parts:

# - "calculate_average" function definition: high
weight

# - "numbers" parameter: high weight

# - "total" variable: medium weight

# - "for" loop: high weight

# - "len(numbers)": high weight
```

```
# Based on these weights, the transformer
understands the context and can generate related
code.
```

In practice, the attention mechanism is implemented using matrix operations. The transformer calculates "queries," "keys," and "values" for each word or code element, and then uses these to compute attention scores.

While we won't go into the detailed math here, it's important to understand that this attention mechanism is what allows transformers to capture long-range dependencies and understand complex relationships.

This ability to understand context is what makes transformers so powerful for code generation. They can understand the overall structure of a program and generate code that fits seamlessly into that structure.

For example, if we give a transformer a prompt like "Write a function to sort a list of strings," it can not only generate the code for the function but also understand the context in which the function will be used.

Here's a simple Python example of how we might use a pre-trained transformer for code generation:

```python
Python

import transformers

model_name = "Salesforce/codegen-350M-multi" #
Example model

tokenizer =
transformers.AutoTokenizer.from_pretrained(model_
name)
```

```
model =
transformers.AutoModelForCausalLM.from_pretrained
(model_name)

prompt = "def sort_strings(strings):"

inputs = tokenizer.encode(prompt,
return_tensors="pt")

outputs = model.generate(inputs, max_length=100,
num_return_sequences=1, temperature=0.2)

generated_code = tokenizer.decode(outputs[0],
skip_special_tokens=True)

print(generated_code)
```

In this example, we're using the transformers library to load a pre-trained code generation model and generate code based on a prompt. This demonstrates the practical application of transformers in code generation.

In summary, neural networks and, more specifically, transformers are the backbone of modern generative AI. Their ability to understand context and generate coherent output makes them incredibly powerful tools for code generation. While the underlying math can be complex, understanding the basic principles allows us to use these tools effectively.

2.2 Language Models for Code Generation

Let's switch gears a bit and talk about language models, specifically how they're used to generate code. Now, you might be thinking, "Language models? Aren't those for text?" And you're right, they are. But here's the thing: code is also a language, just with a different set of rules and a different vocabulary.

Think about it. Both natural languages and programming languages have syntax, grammar, and semantics. They both have rules that dictate how words or code elements can be combined to form meaningful expressions. This is why we can adapt language models to understand and generate code.

The fundamental idea is that we can train a language model on a massive dataset of code, just like we train it on a dataset of text. The model learns the patterns and structures of different programming languages, and it learns how to generate code that follows those patterns and structures.

Now, how does this work in practice? Well, these models use the same transformer architecture we talked about earlier. They process the input sequence, which can be text or code, and generate the output sequence, which is also text or code.

Let's take a simple example. Suppose we want to generate a Python function that calculates the sum of a list of numbers.

We might give the language model a prompt like this:

```
Python

# Function to calculate the sum of a list of
numbers

def sum_list(numbers):
```

The language model, having been trained on a vast dataset of Python code, can then predict what comes next.

It might generate something like this:

```
Python

def sum_list(numbers):
```

```
"""

    Calculates the sum of a list of numbers.

    """

    total = 0

    for number in numbers:

        total += number

    return total
```

Notice how the model not only generates the core logic of the function but also includes a docstring. This is because it has learned from the many examples of well-documented code in its training data.

Now, let's break down how the model actually generates this code. It works by predicting the next token in the sequence. A token can be a word, a character, or a piece of code.

In this example, the model might predict the following sequence of tokens:

"def", " ", "sum_list", "(", "numbers", ")", ":", "\n", " ", " " ", " ", " ", "\"", " ", " ", " ", " ", "Calculates", " ", "the", " ", "sum", " " ", "of", " ", "a", " ", "list", " ", "of", " ", "numbers", ".", "\"", "\n", no " ", " ", " ", " ", "total", " ", "=", " ", "o", "\n", " ", " ", " ", " ", "for", " ", "number", " ", "in", " ", "numbers", ":", "\n", " ", " ", " ", " ", " ", " ", " ", " ", "total", " ", "+=", " ", "number", "\n", " ", " ", " ", " ", "return", " ", "total"

The model generates this sequence of tokens one by one, based on the previous tokens in the sequence. It uses its understanding of the Python language to predict the most likely next token.

This process is called "autoregressive generation," because the model generates each token based on the tokens that came before it. This is similar to how we generate text when we write or speak.

Now, you might be wondering, "How does the model know which tokens to generate?" Well, it uses its learned patterns and structures to make predictions. It assigns probabilities to different tokens and chooses the most likely one.

For example, after generating the token "def," the model might assign a high probability to the token "sum_list," because it knows that function definitions in Python typically start with the keyword "def" followed by the function name.

This process is repeated for each token in the sequence, until the model generates the entire code snippet.

Now, let's look at a more complex example. Suppose we want to generate a function that reads data from a CSV file and performs some data processing.

We might give the language model a prompt like this:

```Python

# Function to read data from a CSV file and
process it

import pandas as pd



def process_csv(filename):
```

The language model might generate something like this:

```Python
```

```python
def process_csv(filename):

    """

    Reads data from a CSV file, performs some
data processing, and returns the processed data.

    """

    df = pd.read_csv(filename)

    # Perform some data processing here

    df['processed_data'] = df['column1'] * 2

    return df
```

In this example, the model has used the pandas library, which is a common tool for data processing in Python. It has also added a basic data processing step. This shows how it can understand and use external libraries and complex data structures.

It's important to understand that these models aren't just copying and pasting code. They're learning the underlying patterns and structures of code, allowing them to generate new and original code. This is what makes them so powerful.

We can also fine-tune these models on smaller datasets to make them more specialized for specific tasks. For example, if we want to generate code for a specific library or framework, we can fine-tune the model on a dataset of code that uses that library or framework.

This allows us to create models that are highly specialized and effective for specific coding tasks.

In summary, language models for code generation are powerful tools that can help us write code more efficiently and creatively.

They use the same transformer architecture as language models for text, but they're trained on massive datasets of code. They learn the patterns and structures of different programming languages, and they can generate new and original code based on our prompts. They are a game changer in the world of code.

2.3 Training Generative AI Models

Alright, let's talk about what goes on behind the scenes to make these generative AI models work: training. It's a complex process, but understanding the basics can really help us appreciate the power of these tools.

To begin, the core idea is that we're teaching the model to understand patterns and relationships in data. In our case, that data is code. We feed the model massive datasets of code, and it learns to predict the next token in a sequence.

Think of it like teaching a child a new language. You show them examples of sentences, and they learn the grammar and vocabulary. In the same way, we show the model examples of code, and it learns the syntax and semantics of programming languages.

The process involves several key steps. First, we need to gather a large dataset of code. This dataset might include code from open-source repositories, code snippets from websites, and even generated code. The larger and more diverse the dataset, the better the model will be at generating code.

Once we have the dataset, we need to preprocess it. This involves cleaning the code, removing any irrelevant information, and tokenizing it. Tokenization is the process of breaking the code into smaller units, such as words, characters, or code elements.

For example, consider the following Python code:

```Python
```

```
def add_numbers(a, b):

    return a + b
```

After tokenization, it might look like this:

["def", "add_numbers", "(", "a", ",", "b", ")", ":",
"return", "a", "+", "b"]

Each of these elements is a token.

Next, we feed the tokenized code into the neural network. As we discussed earlier, we typically use transformer networks due to their ability to handle sequential data. The network processes the code and generates predictions for the next token in the sequence.

Let's illustrate this with a simplified example. Suppose we're training the model on the Python code above. We would feed the model the first few tokens and ask it to predict the next one. For instance, if we feed it ["def", "add_numbers", "("], the model might predict "a".

The model then compares its prediction to the actual next token and adjusts its internal parameters, or weights, to minimize the difference. This process is called "backpropagation." It's essentially how the model learns from its mistakes.

We repeat this process for every sequence of tokens in the dataset. The model gradually learns to predict the next token with increasing accuracy.

A crucial concept here is the "loss function." This function measures the difference between the model's predictions and the actual tokens. The goal of training is to minimize this loss function.

For example, a common loss function for language models is "cross-entropy loss." It measures the difference between the probability distribution of the model's predictions and the actual probability distribution of the next tokens.

The training process requires a lot of computational power and time. We're talking about processing massive datasets and adjusting millions of parameters. This is why training these models often requires specialized hardware like GPUs or TPUs.

Once the model is trained, we can use it for code generation. We give it a prompt, and it generates code based on its learned patterns.

However, the model's performance depends heavily on the quality and diversity of the training data. If the data is biased or incomplete, the model might generate code that reflects those biases or limitations.

For example, if the model is trained primarily on code written by male developers, it might generate code that reflects gender biases.

That's why it's crucial to carefully curate the training data and to use techniques like data augmentation to improve the model's performance.

Data augmentation involves creating variations of the training data to increase its diversity. For example, we might randomly shuffle the order of code snippets or replace certain code elements with synonyms.

We can also fine-tune pre-trained models on smaller datasets to make them more specialized for specific tasks. Fine-tuning involves continuing the training process on a smaller, more focused dataset.

For example, if we want to generate code for a specific library or framework, we can fine-tune the model on a dataset of code that uses that library or framework.

This allows us to create models that are highly specialized and effective for specific coding tasks.

Let's look at a practical example. Suppose we want to fine-tune a pre-trained model to generate code for the pandas library. We might create a dataset of Python code that uses pandas for data processing.

Then, we would continue the training process on this dataset, adjusting the model's parameters to improve its performance on pandas-related code.

Here's a simplified conceptual example of how fine-tuning might work:

```python
Python


import transformers



model_name = "Salesforce/codegen-350M-multi" # Example model

tokenizer = transformers.AutoTokenizer.from_pretrained(model_name)

model = transformers.AutoModelForCausalLM.from_pretrained(model_name)



# Assuming we have a dataset of pandas-related code: pandas_dataset
```

```
for batch in pandas_dataset:

    inputs = tokenizer.encode(batch,
return_tensors="pt")

    outputs = model(inputs, labels=inputs)

    loss = outputs.loss

    loss.backward()

    # Update model parameters based on the loss
```

This is a very simplified example, but it illustrates the basic idea of fine-tuning.

In summary, training generative AI models for code generation involves a complex process of feeding massive datasets of code into neural networks and adjusting their parameters to minimize the difference between predictions and actual tokens. We can also fine-tune pre-trained models on smaller datasets to make them more specialized for specific tasks. The success of these models depends heavily on the quality and diversity of the training data.

2.4 Understanding Model Architectures (Codex, CodeT5, etc.)

Let's get into the specifics of some of the model architectures that are making waves in code generation. It's not just about knowing they exist, but understanding their strengths and how they operate. This knowledge is crucial for us as developers, so we can make informed choices about which tools to use.

We've talked about transformers, and they form the base of many of these models. However, there are nuances to how they're applied and trained that lead to different capabilities.

First, let's discuss Codex. You've likely heard of it, and it's a very powerful tool. Codex is essentially a descendant of the GPT series, but it's been fine-tuned on a massive dataset of publicly available code, especially from GitHub.[1] This fine-tuning is what makes it so proficient at generating code.

What's important to understand about Codex is its focus. It's really optimized for generating code based on natural language descriptions. This means you can give it a prompt like, "Write a Python function to sort a list of strings," and it will generate the code for you.

Here's an example of how you might interact with Codex through an API, if one were available for direct user access (currently, it is primarily integrated into products like GitHub Copilot):

```python
Python

# Conceptual example of interacting with Codex
API (not real code, for illustrative purposes)

import requests



def generate_code_with_codex(prompt):

    api_url =
"https://codex-api.example.com/generate"

    headers = {"Authorization": "Bearer
YOUR_API_KEY"}

    data = {"prompt": prompt}
```

```python
    response = requests.post(api_url,
headers=headers, json=data)


    if response.status_code == 200:

        return response.json()["generated_code"]

    else:

        return "Error: " + response.text


# Example usage

prompt = "def sort_list_of_strings(strings):"

generated_code = generate_code_with_codex(prompt)

print(generated_code)
```

The model behind Codex is trained to understand the context of the prompt and generate code that matches the intent.[2] It's particularly good at generating code in languages like Python, JavaScript, and other popular languages.[3]

Codex excels at tasks like:

- Generating function implementations based on docstrings.
- Completing code snippets and suggesting code completions.
- Translating natural language descriptions into code.

Now, let's shift our focus to CodeT5. This is another powerful architecture, but it has a slightly different approach. CodeT5 is based on the T5 model, which is a text-to-text transformer.[4] This means it can handle both text and code as input and output.

What's unique about CodeT5 is its ability to understand the relationship between code and natural language. It's trained on a dataset of code and natural language descriptions, which allows it to perform tasks like code summarization, code translation, and code generation.[5]

For instance, you can give CodeT5 a code snippet and ask it to generate a natural language summary of the code. Or, you can give it a natural language description and ask it to generate the corresponding code.

Here's a conceptual Python example using the transformers library to load a CodeT5 model and generate code:

```python
Python


import transformers



model_name = "Salesforce/codet5-base" # Example
model

tokenizer =
transformers.AutoTokenizer.from_pretrained(model_
name)

model =
transformers.AutoModelForSeq2SeqLM.from_pretraine
d(model_name)



prompt = "Translate this Python function to
JavaScript: def calculate_area(length, width):
return length * width"
```

```
inputs = tokenizer.encode(prompt,
return_tensors="pt")

outputs = model.generate(inputs, max_length=200)

generated_code = tokenizer.decode(outputs[0],
skip_special_tokens=True)

print(generated_code)
```

CodeT5 shines in tasks like:

- Code summarization and documentation generation.
- Code translation between different programming languages.
- Generating code based on natural language descriptions.

It's important to understand that these models are constantly evolving. New architectures and techniques are being developed all the time.

For example, there are models that are specifically designed for code completion in IDEs, and there are models that are being used to generate code for domain-specific languages.

When we consider which model architecture to use, we should think about the task at hand. If we need to generate code based on natural language descriptions, Codex or a similar model might be a good choice. If we need to perform tasks like code summarization or translation, CodeT5 might be more suitable.

It's also important to consider the limitations of these models. They're not perfect, and they can sometimes generate code that is incorrect or inefficient.[6] We need to use them responsibly and critically evaluate the generated code.

In essence, understanding the nuances of different model architectures allows us to leverage these tools more effectively. We can choose the right tool for the job and use it to enhance our coding abilities.

Chapter 3: Setting Up Your AI Coding Environment

This chapter is all about getting you ready to work with generative AI. Don't worry, we'll take it step by step, and by the end, you'll be ready to start experimenting.

3.1 Installing Necessary Tools and Libraries

Alright, let's get our coding environment ready to handle generative AI. This first step is all about making sure we have the right tools in place. It might seem a bit like setting up a workshop, but trust me, having a well-organized workspace makes all the difference.

When we're working with generative AI, especially for code, we're going to be dealing with Python a lot. It's become the go-to language for many AI applications due to its extensive library support and ease of use. So, the first thing we need is a solid Python setup.

Now, if you're a seasoned developer, you probably have Python installed already. But for those who are new to it, or if you want a clean environment, I recommend using Anaconda. Anaconda is a distribution of Python that comes with a bunch of pre-installed libraries and tools, making it super convenient for data science and AI work. It also helps with managing different Python environments, which is crucial when working on multiple projects.

Let's say you're installing Anaconda. You'd head over to the Anaconda website, download the installer for your operating system (Windows, macOS, or Linux), and run it. The installer will guide you through the process, and you'll have Python and a bunch of useful libraries ready to go.

Once we have Python sorted, we need to think about the libraries that will allow us to interact with AI models. We're going to be dealing with APIs, which are like communication channels between our code and the AI models.

For making those API calls, we'll use the requests library. This library is fantastic for sending HTTP requests, which is how we'll be talking to the AI models. Think of it as a tool that allows our Python code to send messages over the internet.

To install requests, we'll use pip, the Python package installer.

Open your terminal or command prompt and type:

Bash

pip install requests

Pip will download and install the requests library, and it'll be ready to use in our Python scripts.

Now, let's talk about transformer models. We've discussed how powerful they are for code generation. If we want to work with pre-trained transformer models directly, we'll need the transformers library from Hugging Face. Hugging Face is a company that's doing amazing work in making AI models accessible.

To install the transformers library, we'll use pip again:

Bash

pip install transformers

This will download and install the library, along with the necessary dependencies. With this library, we'll be able to load pre-trained models, tokenize text and code, and generate code.

Here's a simple example of how we might use the transformers library to load a pre-trained model:

Python

```
import transformers



model_name = "Salesforce/codegen-350M-multi"   #
Example model

tokenizer =
transformers.AutoTokenizer.from_pretrained(model_
name)

model =
transformers.AutoModelForCausalLM.from_pretrained
(model_name)



print("Model loaded successfully!")
```

In this example, we're loading a pre-trained code generation model. The AutoTokenizer and AutoModelForCausalLM classes automatically select the appropriate classes for the model based on its name.

Now, let's talk about virtual environments. If you're working on multiple projects, you'll want to keep their dependencies separate. This prevents conflicts and makes it easier to manage your projects.

Virtual environments are like isolated boxes where you can install libraries without affecting your system's Python installation. You can create a virtual environment using the venv module, which is part of Python.

Here's how you can create a virtual environment called "myenv":

Bash

python -m venv myenv

This will create a directory called "myenv" with the necessary files for the virtual environment.

To activate the virtual environment, you'll need to run a command specific to your operating system.

On Windows:[1]

Bash

myenv\Scripts\activate

On macOS and Linux:

Bash

source myenv/bin/activate

Once the virtual environment is activated,[2] you'll see its name in your terminal prompt. Any libraries you install will be installed within the virtual environment.

Let's say we want to install the requests library within our virtual environment.

We can use pip as before:

Bash

pip install requests

This will install the library in the virtual environment, and it won't affect our system's Python installation.

By using virtual environments, we can keep our projects organized and avoid dependency conflicts.

Now, if you're using a specific AI model or service that requires its own library or SDK, you'll need to install that as well. Always refer to the documentation for the specific model or service you're using.

For example, if you're using a cloud-based AI service, they might provide a Python SDK that you can install using pip.

In essence, setting up our coding environment is about getting the right tools and libraries in place and keeping our projects organized. It's like preparing our workspace before we start building something amazing.

3.2 Interacting with Generative AI APIs

Alright, let's get into the practical side of things: how we actually talk to these generative AI models. We're going to be using APIs, and understanding how they work is crucial to getting the most out of these powerful tools.

Think of an API as a messenger. It's the middleman that allows our code to send requests to an AI model and receive responses. Just like how you might order food at a restaurant by giving your order to a waiter, we send our "orders" or "requests" to the AI model through the API.

Most AI models are accessed via web APIs, which means we send our requests over the internet using the HTTP protocol. If you've done any web development, you're probably already familiar with HTTP. It's the same protocol that your web browser uses to fetch web pages.

We're going to use Python and the requests library to interact with these APIs. The requests library makes it easy to send HTTP requests and handle the responses.

Let's start with a basic example. Suppose we want to use an AI model to generate code based on a prompt.

We might send a request to the API like this:

```python
Python

import requests

import json


def generate_code(prompt, api_key):
    api_url = "https://api.example-ai.com/generate_code"
    headers = {
        "Authorization": f"Bearer {api_key}",
        "Content-Type": "application/json"
    }
    data = {"prompt": prompt}

    try:
        response = requests.post(api_url, headers=headers, json=data)
```

```python
        response.raise_for_status()  # Raise
HTTPError for bad responses (4xx or 5xx)

        return response.json()["generated_code"]

    except requests.exceptions.RequestException
as e:

        return f"Error: {e}"


# Example usage (replace with your actual API
key)

api_key = "YOUR_API_KEY"

prompt = "def sort_list(my_list):"

generated_code = generate_code(prompt, api_key)

print(generated_code)
```

In this example, we're sending a POST request to the API endpoint https://api.example-ai.com/generate_code. We're including our prompt in the request body as a JSON object. We're also including an API key in the headers for authentication.

The API then returns the generated code as a JSON response. We're using the response.json() method to parse the JSON response and extract the generated code.

It's crucial to understand the API documentation for the specific model you're using. It will tell you how to format your requests, what parameters are available, and how to interpret the responses.

Here are some key aspects to consider when interacting with AI APIs:

- Authentication: Most APIs require you to authenticate your requests using an API key or other credentials. You'll need to include these credentials in the headers of your requests.
- Request Methods: APIs typically use different HTTP methods to perform different actions. The most common methods are GET, POST, PUT, and DELETE. For code generation, we'll usually use POST requests.
- Request Body: The request body contains the data that we're sending to the API. In our case, it will usually contain the prompt that we want the AI model to use.
- Response Body: The response body contains the data that the API is sending back to us. In our case, it will usually contain the generated code or text.
- Error Handling: It's important to handle errors gracefully when interacting with APIs. This includes handling HTTP errors, network errors, and API-specific errors.

Let's look at a slightly more complex example. Suppose we want to use an AI model to translate code from Python to JavaScript.

We might send a request to the API like this:

```python
Python

import requests

import json



def translate_code(code, source_lang,
target_lang, api_key):

    api_url =
"https://api.example-ai.com/translate_code"
```

```python
    headers = {
        "Authorization": f"Bearer {api_key}",
        "Content-Type": "application/json"
    }
    data = {
        "code": code,
        "source_lang": source_lang,
        "target_lang": target_lang
    }


    try:
        response = requests.post(api_url,
headers=headers, json=data)
        response.raise_for_status()
        return response.json()["translated_code"]
    except requests.exceptions.RequestException
as e:
        return f"Error: {e}"


# Example usage
api_key = "YOUR_API_KEY"
```

```
python_code = "def calculate_area(length, width):
return length * width"

javascript_code = translate_code(python_code,
"python", "javascript", api_key)

print(javascript_code)
```

In this example, we're sending a POST request to the API endpoint https://api.example-ai.com/translate_code. We're including the code to translate, the source language, and the target language in the request body.

This example shows how we can use APIs to perform more complex tasks with AI models.

It's important to note that the specific details of how you interact with an API will depend on the API you're using. Always refer to the API documentation for the most accurate and up-to-date information.

By understanding how to interact with AI APIs, we can leverage the power of these models in our coding projects. It's like having a powerful assistant that can help us with a wide range of coding tasks.

3.3 Managing API Keys and Rate Limits

Let's talk about something that's absolutely crucial when working with AI APIs: managing API keys and handling rate limits. This might not be the most exciting topic, but it's essential for building robust and reliable applications. Think of it as setting up the security and traffic control for our coding projects.

First, let's discuss API keys. These keys are like digital passwords that give you access to the AI model's services. They're unique to you, and they allow the API provider to track your usage and bill you accordingly.

It's absolutely vital to keep your API keys secure. Never, ever hardcode them directly into your code. If you accidentally share your code, you'll also be sharing your API key, and anyone can use it.

A much better approach is to store your API keys in environment variables. Environment variables are variables that are set in your operating system, and they're a secure way to store sensitive information.

Here's how you can access an API key from an environment variable in Python:

```python
Python

import os


api_key = os.environ.get("MY_API_KEY")


if api_key:

    print("API key found!")

else:

    print("API key not found.")
```

You can set environment variables in your operating system's settings or in your terminal.

For example, on macOS and Linux, you can use the export command:

Bash

```bash
export MY_API_KEY="your_actual_api_key"
```

On Windows, you can use the set command:

Bash

```bash
set MY_API_KEY="your_actual_api_key"
```

By storing your API keys in environment variables, you keep them separate from your code, which is much safer.

Another good practice is to use a configuration file to store your API keys and other settings. You can use a file format like JSON or YAML, which is easy to read and write.

Here's an example of how you might use a JSON file to store your API key:

JSON

```json
{
    "api_key": "your_actual_api_key"
}
```

And here's how you can read the API key from the JSON file in Python:

Python

```python
import json
```

```python
def get_api_key(filepath="config.json"):

    try:

        with open(filepath, "r") as f:

            config = json.load(f)

            return config["api_key"]

    except FileNotFoundError:

        return None


api_key = get_api_key()


if api_key:

    print("API key found!")

else:

    print("API key not found.")
```

This approach is especially useful when you have multiple settings to manage.

Now, let's talk about rate limits. These are limits on the number of requests you can make to the API in a given time period. They're put in place to prevent abuse and to ensure that the API can handle the load.

If you exceed the rate limit, you'll receive an error message, typically an HTTP 429 "Too Many Requests" error. It's crucial to handle these errors gracefully in your code.

A common technique for handling rate limits is exponential backoff. This involves waiting for increasing amounts of time before retrying the request.

Here's a simplified example of how you might implement exponential backoff in Python:

```python
Python

import requests

import time


def generate_code_with_retry(prompt, api_key,
max_retries=5):

    retries = 0

    while retries < max_retries:

        response = requests.post(


"https://api.example-ai.com/generate_code",

            headers={"Authorization": f"Bearer
{api_key}"},

            json={"prompt": prompt}

        )



        if response.status_code == 200:
```

```python
        return
response.json()["generated_code"]

    elif response.status_code == 429:

        retries += 1

        wait_time = 2 ** retries  #
Exponential backoff

            print(f"Rate limit exceeded. Retrying
in {wait_time} seconds.")

            time.sleep(wait_time)

    else:

        return f"Error:
{response.status_code} - {response.text}"


    return "Error: Max retries exceeded."
```

In this example, we're retrying the request up to five times, waiting for increasing amounts of time between retries.

It's also a good idea to check the API documentation for the specific rate limits. Some APIs provide headers that indicate the remaining time until the rate limit resets. You can use this information to implement more sophisticated rate limiting strategies.

Here's an example of how you might check for rate limit headers:

```python
Python

response = requests.post(
```

```python
    "https://api.example-ai.com/generate_code",

    headers={"Authorization": f"Bearer
{api_key}"},

    json={"prompt": prompt}

)



if "X-RateLimit-Remaining" in response.headers:

    remaining =
response.headers["X-RateLimit-Remaining"]

    print(f"Rate limit remaining: {remaining}")



if "X-RateLimit-Reset" in response.headers:

    reset_time =
response.headers["X-RateLimit-Reset"]

    print(f"Rate limit reset time: {reset_time}")
```

By understanding how to manage API keys and handle rate limits, we can build applications that are both secure and reliable. It's about being a responsible developer and ensuring that we're using these powerful tools in a sustainable way.

3.4 Best Practices for Setup

Okay, let's wrap up this chapter by talking about some best practices for setting up your AI coding environment. It's not just about getting the tools installed; it's about setting up a workflow that's efficient, secure, and maintainable. Think of it as organizing your workspace so you can focus on building amazing things.

First and foremost, always use virtual environments. We touched on this earlier, but it's worth emphasizing. Virtual environments are like isolated containers for your project's dependencies. They allow you to install libraries and packages without affecting your system's Python installation. This is crucial for avoiding conflicts and ensuring that your projects are reproducible.

Imagine you're working on two projects. One project uses an older version of a library, and the other uses a newer version. Without virtual environments, you'd have to constantly switch between versions, which can be a real headache. With virtual environments, you can have each project in its own isolated environment, with its own set of dependencies.

Here's a quick reminder of how to create and activate a virtual environment using venv:

Bash

Create a virtual environment called "myenv"

python -m venv myenv

Activate the virtual environment

On Windows:

myenv\Scripts\activate

On macOS and Linux:

source myenv/bin/activate

Once the virtual environment is activated,[1] any libraries you install will be installed within the environment, and they won't affect your system's Python installation.

Next, let's talk about managing dependencies. It's good practice to keep track of the libraries your project uses and their versions. You can do this by creating a requirements.txt file. This file lists all the libraries your project depends on, along with their versions.

Here's an example of a requirements.txt file:

requests==2.26.0

transformers==4.11.3

You can generate a requirements.txt file from your virtual environment using pip:

Bash

```
pip freeze > requirements.txt
```

And you can install the dependencies from a requirements.txt file using pip:

Bash

```
pip install -r requirements.txt
```

Using a requirements.txt file makes it easy to set up your project on a new machine or share it with others.

Now, let's talk about version control. If you're not already using version control, like Git, you should start. Version control allows you to track changes to your code, collaborate with others, and easily revert to previous versions.[2]

Think of it like a time machine for your code. If you make a mistake, you can easily go back to a previous version. If you're working with a team, you can use Git to merge your changes and avoid conflicts.

Here's a basic example of how to initialize a Git repository:

Bash

git init

And here's how to add and commit your changes:

Bash

git add .

git commit -m "Initial commit"

Using Git is a fundamental skill for any developer, and it's especially important when working on AI projects, which can involve a lot of experimentation and iteration.

Another crucial best practice is to keep your code organized. Use meaningful variable and function names, write comments to explain complex logic, and break your code into smaller, reusable functions.

This makes your code easier to read and understand, both for yourself and for others. It also makes it easier to debug and maintain.

Let's look at an example. Instead of writing a long, complex function, break it down into smaller, more manageable functions:

Python

```python
def calculate_average(numbers):

    total = sum(numbers)

    return total / len(numbers)


def process_data(data):

    filtered_data = [x for x in data if x > 10]

    average = calculate_average(filtered_data)

    return average
```

This code is much easier to read and understand than a single, long function.

And finally, document your code and your setup. This includes writing docstrings for your functions, creating README files for your projects, and documenting any specific setup instructions.

Documentation is crucial for making your code accessible to others and for ensuring that your projects are maintainable.

Think of it like writing a user manual for your code. It helps others understand how to use your code and how to set up their environment.

Here's an example of a docstring for a Python function:

```
Python
```

```python
def calculate_average(numbers):

    """

    Calculates the average of a list of numbers.
```

```
    Args:

        numbers (list): A list of numbers.


    Returns:

        float: The average of the numbers.

    """

    total = sum(numbers)

    return total / len(numbers)
```

By following these best practices, you'll be well on your way to building robust and maintainable AI-powered applications. It's about setting yourself up for success and creating a coding environment that's both efficient and enjoyable.

Chapter 4: Code Generation Fundamentals

This chapter is all about the fundamentals, the core skills you'll use day-to-day. We're going to talk about crafting effective prompts, exploring some powerful prompting techniques, and looking at real-world examples to see how it all comes together.

4.1 Writing Effective Prompts

Okay, let's talk about the heart of getting generative AI to do what we want: writing effective prompts. In a way, it's like learning to speak a new language, the language of AI instructions. And just like with any language, clarity and precision are paramount.

Think of a prompt as your direct communication with the AI model. It's the set of instructions and context you provide to guide its code generation. The quality of your prompt directly determines the quality of the code you get back. A vague or ambiguous prompt will likely result in code that's equally vague and unusable.

It's a bit like asking a colleague to do something. If you give them a very general instruction, they might not know exactly what you want. But if you give them very specific and detailed instructions, they're more likely to deliver what you need.

Let's start with a simple example. Suppose you want the AI to generate a Python function that calculates the area of a rectangle.

A poor prompt might be:

"Write a function to calculate the area."

This prompt is too general. The AI doesn't know:

- Which programming language to use.

- What the function should be called.
- What the inputs and outputs should be.
- What formula to use.

A much better prompt would be:

"Write a Python function called calculate_rectangle_area that takes the length and width of a rectangle as float inputs and returns the area of the rectangle as a float. Use the formula: area = length * width."

This prompt is much more specific. It tells the AI:

- The programming language (Python).
- The function name (calculate_rectangle_area).
- The data types of the inputs (float).
- The data type of the output (float).
- The formula to use.

With this improved prompt, the AI is much more likely to generate the code you actually need.

Here are some key principles to keep in mind when writing prompts for code generation:

1. Specify the Programming Language

Always explicitly mention the programming language you want the AI to use. This eliminates ambiguity and ensures that the AI generates code in the correct syntax.

For example:

- "Write a JavaScript function..."
- "Generate a C++ class..."
- "Create a Python script..."

2. Be Specific About the Task

Clearly and precisely describe what you want the function or code to do. Avoid vague terms and provide as much detail as possible.

For example:

- Instead of: "Write a function to process data."
- Use: "Write a Python function that takes a list of dictionaries as input and returns a new list of dictionaries with a new key 'processed_value' calculated as the square of the 'value' key."

3. Define Inputs and Outputs

Clearly specify the data types and formats of the inputs and outputs of the function or code. This helps the AI understand how to handle the data.

For example:

- "The function should take an integer as input..."
- "The function should return a string..."
- "The function should accept a list of floats..."
- "The function should output a JSON object..."

4. Provide Context

Give the AI any relevant context that might help it understand the task. This could include information about the application, the domain, or the libraries or frameworks you're using.

For example:

- "In a web application, write a JavaScript function..."
- "Using the pandas library, write a Python function..."
- "For a game development project, write a C++ class..."

5. Use Clear and Concise Language

Avoid jargon, technical terms, and ambiguous words. Write in simple, straightforward language that the AI can easily understand.

For example:

- Instead of: "Implement a recursive algorithm for binary search."
- Use: "Write a function that searches for a value in a sorted list using a recursive approach."

6. Give Examples (If Possible)

Providing examples of input and output can be extremely helpful, especially for complex tasks. This allows the AI to learn from patterns and generate code that matches your desired behavior.

For example:

"Write a Python function that converts a date string from 'YYYY-MM-DD' format to 'DD/MM/YYYY' format.

Example:

Input: '2023-10-27', Output: '27/10/2023'"

Let's look at a more comprehensive example. Suppose you want the AI to generate a function that calculates the Fibonacci sequence up to a given number of terms.

A good prompt would be:

"Write a Python function called fibonacci_sequence that takes an integer n as input and returns a list containing the first n Fibonacci numbers. The Fibonacci sequence[1] starts with 0 and 1, and each subsequent number is the sum of the previous two. For example,[2] if n is 5, the function should return [0, 1, 1, 2, 3]."

This prompt is very specific and provides all the necessary information for the AI to generate the correct code.

In essence, writing effective prompts is about being clear, concise, and specific. It's about providing the AI with enough information to understand your intent and generate the code you need. As you practice, you'll develop a "prompt engineering" intuition, and you'll be able to get the AI to do some pretty amazing things.

4.2 Prompting Techniques (Few-Shot, Chain-of-Thought)

Okay, we've covered the basics of writing clear and specific prompts. Now, let's explore some more advanced techniques that can significantly boost the quality and effectiveness of our code generation: few-shot learning and chain-of-thought prompting. These are like "power-ups" for your prompt engineering skills, allowing you to coax even better results from generative AI.

Few-Shot Learning

Few-shot learning is a technique where you provide the AI with a small number of examples to guide its generation.[1] It's similar to how we teach someone by showing them a few worked examples before asking them to solve a similar problem.

Think of it this way: instead of just giving the AI a general instruction, you give it a few demonstrations. This helps the AI understand the pattern or relationship you want it to capture.

Let's illustrate this with an example. Suppose you want the AI to generate a function that converts a date string from one format to another. Instead of just describing the conversion, you can provide a few examples:

Date conversion:

Input: "2023-10-27", Output: "27/10/2023"

Input: "2024-01-15", Output: "15/01/2024"

Input: "2023-12-03", Output: "03/12/2023"

Write a Python function called `convert_date_format` that takes a date string in "YYYY-MM-DD" format as input and returns the date string in "DD/MM/YYYY" format.

By providing these three examples, you're giving the AI a clear understanding of the desired conversion. It can see the pattern of how the year, month, and day are rearranged.

Here's a breakdown of why this is effective:

- Pattern Recognition: AI models excel at identifying patterns.[2] By giving a few examples, you help the model recognize the underlying logic of the task.
- Contextual Guidance: Examples provide context that might be difficult to express in words. They show the specific input and output formats, which reduces ambiguity.
- Style and Conventions: Examples can also guide the AI to generate code that matches a particular style or set of conventions.[3]

Let's look at another example. Imagine you want the AI to generate a function that extracts the file extension from a filename:

File extension extraction:

Input: "document.txt", Output: "txt"

Input: "image.jpg", Output: "jpg"

Input: "code.py", Output: "py"

Write a Python function called `get_file_extension` that takes a filename as a string input and returns the file extension as a string.

These examples help the AI understand that the file extension is the part of the filename after the last dot.

It's important to note that the number of examples you need will vary depending on the complexity of the task. For simple tasks, a few examples might be enough. For more complex tasks, you might need to provide more examples.

Chain-of-Thought Prompting

Chain-of-thought prompting is another powerful technique that encourages the AI to "think step-by-step" before generating code.[4] This is particularly useful for tasks that involve reasoning or multiple steps.

Instead of directly asking the AI to generate the final code, you guide it through the intermediate steps it needs to take to solve the problem. This helps the AI break down the task into smaller, more manageable parts.

Let's say you want the AI to generate a function that calculates the nth Fibonacci number.

You could use a chain-of-thought prompt like this:

To calculate the nth Fibonacci number, we need to consider the following:

The first two Fibonacci numbers are 0 and 1.

Each subsequent Fibonacci number is the sum of the previous two numbers.

For example:

The 1st Fibonacci number is 0.

The 2nd Fibonacci number is 1.

The 3rd Fibonacci number is 0 + 1 = 1.

The 4th Fibonacci number is 1 + 1 = 2.

The 5th Fibonacci number is 1 + 2 = 3.

Write a Python function called `fibonacci` that takes an integer n as input and returns the nth Fibonacci number.

By explicitly outlining the steps involved in calculating the Fibonacci sequence, you help the AI understand the logic and generate more accurate code.

Here's why chain-of-thought prompting is beneficial:

- Improved Reasoning: It encourages the AI to reason through the problem step-by-step, rather than trying to generate the final code in one go.
- Reduced Errors: By breaking down the task, you can help the AI avoid common errors and generate more robust code.[5]
- Increased Transparency: It makes the AI's reasoning process more transparent, which can help you understand how it arrived at the generated code.

Let's consider another example. Imagine you want the AI to generate a function that sorts a list of strings by their length:

To sort a list of strings by their length, we need to consider the following:

We need to compare the length of each string in the list.

We need to arrange the strings in ascending order of their length.

For example:

Input: ["apple", "banana", "kiwi", "orange"]

Output: ["kiwi", "apple", "orange", "banana"]

Write a Python function called `sort_by_length` that takes a list of strings as input and returns a new list with the strings sorted by their length.

This prompt guides the AI to think about the comparison of string lengths, which is essential for the sorting process.

In essence, few-shot learning and chain-of-thought prompting are powerful techniques that can significantly improve the quality of code generated by AI.[6] They allow you to provide more guidance and context to the AI, leading to more accurate, efficient, and creative code.[7]

4.3 Real-World Code Generation Examples

Okay, so we've covered the theory of writing effective prompts and some advanced techniques. Now, let's bring it all together and see how generative AI can help us with actual coding tasks. I'm going to show you some practical examples that demonstrate the power and versatility of these tools.

First, let's consider a common web development scenario: creating a user registration form. This involves generating HTML for the form's structure and JavaScript for client-side validation.

You could use generative AI to speed up this process.

You might write a prompt like this:

"Generate HTML and JavaScript code for a user registration form with the following fields: username (text input), email (text input), password (password input), and confirm password (password input). Include client-side JavaScript validation to ensure that the email field is a valid email address and that the password and confirm password fields match. Use modern HTML5 features and basic CSS styling for a clean layout."

The AI could then generate code similar to this:

```
HTML

<!DOCTYPE html>

<html lang="en">

<head>

    <meta charset="UTF-8">

    <meta name="viewport"
content="width=device-width, initial-scale=1.0">

    <title>User Registration</title>

    <style>

        form {

            display: flex;
```

```
            flex-direction: column;

            width: 300px;

            margin: 0 auto;

        }

        label {

            margin-top: 10px;

        }

    </style>

</head>

<body>

    <form id="registrationForm">

        <label for="username">Username:</label>

        <input type="text" id="username"
name="username" required>


        <label for="email">Email:</label>

        <input type="email" id="email"
name="email" required>


        <label for="password">Password:</label>

        <input type="password" id="password"
name="password" required>
```

```html
        <label for="confirmPassword">Confirm
Password:</label>

        <input type="password"
id="confirmPassword" name="confirmPassword"
required>


        <button type="submit">Register</button>

    </form>


    <script>
        const form =
document.getElementById('registrationForm');

        const emailInput =
document.getElementById('email');

        const passwordInput =
document.getElementById('password');

        const confirmPasswordInput =
document.getElementById('confirmPassword');


        form.addEventListener('submit',
function(event) {

            let isValid = true;
```

```
        if (!isValidEmail(emailInput.value))
{

            alert('Please enter a valid email
address.');

            isValid = false;

            event.preventDefault();

        }



        if (passwordInput.value !==
confirmPasswordInput.value) {

            alert('Passwords do not match.');

            isValid = false;

            event.preventDefault();

        }



        if (!isValid) {

            event.preventDefault(); //
Prevent form submission if validation fails

        }

    });


    function isValidEmail(email) {
```

```
        const emailRegex =
/^[^\s@]+@[^\s@]+\.[^\s@]+$/;

        return emailRegex.test(email);

    }

  </script>

</body>

</html>
```

This example shows how generative AI can significantly speed up the development of common web components. It saves you from writing all the HTML and JavaScript from scratch, allowing you to focus on the application's logic and user experience.[1]

Now, let's consider a data analysis scenario. Suppose you're working with data in a CSV file and need to perform some processing using the pandas library in Python.

You could use generative AI to generate the code for this task. You might write a prompt like this:

"Generate a Python function using the pandas library to read data from a CSV file named 'data.csv'.

The function should then:

1. Load the CSV file into a pandas DataFrame.
2. Add a new column named 'total_sales' that is the product of the 'quantity' and 'price' columns.
3. Filter the DataFrame to include only rows where the 'category' column is 'Electronics'.
4. Calculate the average 'total_sales' for the 'Electronics' category.
5. Return the calculated average."

The AI might generate code similar to this:

Python

```python
import pandas as pd


def process_sales_data(filename='data.csv'):
    """

    Reads sales data from a CSV file, calculates
total sales,

    filters by category, and returns the average
sales for the

    'Electronics' category.

    """

    try:

        df = pd.read_csv(filename)

        df['total_sales'] = df['quantity'] *
df['price']

        electronics_df = df[df['category'] ==
'Electronics']

        average_electronics_sales =
electronics_df['total_sales'].mean()

        return average_electronics_sales

    except FileNotFoundError:

        return "Error: CSV file not found."
```

```
# Example usage:

average_sales = process_sales_data()

print(f"Average sales for Electronics:
{average_sales}")
```

This example demonstrates how generative AI can help automate data processing tasks, saving you time and effort in writing pandas code. It also showcases how the AI can handle file input, data manipulation, and calculations.

Let's look at one more example, this time in the context of game development. Imagine you're creating a simple game and need to generate code for handling player movement in a 2D environment.

You could use generative AI to generate the code for this.

You might write a prompt like this:

"Generate C# code for Unity that handles player movement in a 2D game. The player should be able to move left, right, up, and down using the arrow keys. The player's movement speed should be a configurable variable. Include collision detection to prevent the player from moving through walls (assume there's a 'Wall' tag on wall objects)."

The AI could generate code similar to this:

```
C#


using UnityEngine;



public class PlayerMovement : MonoBehaviour
```

```csharp
{
    public float moveSpeed = 5f; // Player
movement speed

    private Rigidbody2D rb;


    void Start()

    {

        rb = GetComponent<Rigidbody2D>();

    }



    void FixedUpdate()

    {

        float moveX =
Input.GetAxisRaw("Horizontal");

        float moveY =
Input.GetAxisRaw("Vertical");



        Vector2 movement = new Vector2(moveX,
moveY).normalized * moveSpeed;

        rb.MovePosition(rb.position + movement *
Time.fixedDeltaTime);

    }
```

```
void OnCollisionEnter2D(Collision2D
collision)

    {

        if (collision.gameObject.tag == "Wall")

        {

            // Handle collision with walls (e.g.,
stop movement)

            rb.velocity = Vector2.zero;

        }

    }

}
```

This example shows how generative AI can assist with game development tasks, providing code for common game mechanics.

These examples highlight the potential of generative AI to automate various coding tasks across different domains. By providing clear and specific prompts, you can leverage AI to speed up development, improve code quality, and focus on the more creative and challenging aspects of your work.[2]

Chapter 5: Automating Routine Tasks

Imagine a world where you spend less time setting up the basic structure of a project and more time on the core logic. That's the promise of generative AI for task automation. It's like having a tireless assistant who can handle the repetitive stuff, leaving you to be the architect and the innovator.

5.1 Generating Boilerplate Code

Alright, let's talk about something that every coder knows intimately: boilerplate code. It's that foundational, repetitive code that forms the structure of so many projects. Think of it as the scaffolding of a building; it's necessary to get things started, but you don't want to spend all your time building scaffolding, do you? You want to get to the architecture and the design.

Generative AI offers a real opportunity to offload the burden of boilerplate code. It can act as a diligent assistant, handling the routine setup so we can concentrate on the unique, creative, and problem-solving aspects of development.

So, what exactly *is* boilerplate? It's the code you find yourself writing again and again, with only minor variations. It's the code that establishes the basic structure, the standard procedures. It's often predictable and follows established patterns.

Here are some typical examples where generative AI can be especially helpful:

- Class Definitions: In object-oriented programming, defining classes often involves creating fields (or attributes) and then writing "getter" and "setter" methods to access and modify those fields. This is very repetitive, especially when you have many classes or classes with many attributes.

- CRUD Operations: If your application interacts with a database, you'll need to implement Create, Read, Update, and Delete (CRUD) operations. The fundamental logic is similar for each entity (e.g., users, products, orders), but you change the table and column names.
- API Endpoint Setup: When building web APIs, you need to define routes, handle HTTP requests (GET, POST, etc.), and format responses. The basic structure of the code is often similar across endpoints.
- Data Access Layers: Code that interacts directly with databases (data access layers) often follows patterns for connection management, query execution, and data mapping.
- GUI Element Creation: When building graphical user interfaces, you might need to create similar elements like forms, tables, or lists, with variations in the specific data displayed or actions performed.

Let's explore how generative AI can ease the pain of boilerplate in these scenarios:

1. Generating Class Definitions

Imagine you're developing in Python and need a class to represent a "Book." You'll likely have attributes like title, author, and publication_year. Instead of writing the __init__ method and properties manually, you can ask the AI to generate it.

You could provide a prompt like this:

"Generate a Python class called 'Book' with attributes 'title' (string), 'author' (string), and 'publication_year' (integer). Include an __init__ method to initialize the attributes and properties for accessing them."

The AI could then produce code like this:

Python

```python
class Book:

    def __init__(self, title, author,
    publication_year):

        self.title = title

        self.author = author

        self.publication_year = publication_year


    @property

    def title(self):

        return self._title


    @title.setter

    def title(self, value):

        self._title = value


    @property

    def author(self):

        return self._author


    @author.setter
```

```python
    def author(self, value):

        self._author = value


    @property

    def publication_year(self):

        return self._publication_year


    @publication_year.setter

    def publication_year(self, value):

        self._publication_year = value
```

This saves you the time and effort of writing all those property definitions, allowing you to focus on the core functionality of the Book class.

2. Generating CRUD Operations

Let's say you're building a web application using Django (a Python web framework), and you need to implement CRUD operations for managing "articles."

You could give the AI a prompt like this:

"Generate Django views for creating, retrieving, updating, and deleting 'articles'. An article has a 'title' (string), 'content' (text), and 'publication_date' (date). Use Django's ORM (Object-Relational Mapper) for database interaction."

The AI might generate code similar to this:

Python

```python
from django.shortcuts import render, redirect,
get_object_or_404

from django.http import JsonResponse

from .models import Article

from django.views.decorators.csrf import
csrf_exempt

import json


def article_list(request):

    articles = Article.objects.all()

    data = [{'id': article.id, 'title':
article.title, 'content': article.content,
'publication_date':
str(article.publication_date)} for article in
articles]

    return JsonResponse(data, safe=False)


@csrf_exempt

def article_create(request):

    if request.method == 'POST':

        data = json.loads(request.body)
```

```python
        article =
Article.objects.create(title=data['title'],
content=data['content'],
publication_date=data['publication_date'])

        return JsonResponse({'id': article.id,
'title': article.title, 'content':
article.content, 'publication_date':
str(article.publication_date)}, status=201)

    return JsonResponse({'error': 'Invalid
request method'}, status=400)


def article_detail(request, pk):

    article = get_object_or_404(Article, pk=pk)

    data = {'id': article.id, 'title':
article.title, 'content': article.content,
'publication_date':
str(article.publication_date)}

    return JsonResponse(data)


@csrf_exempt

def article_update(request, pk):

    article = get_object_or_404(Article, pk=pk)

    if request.method == 'PUT':

        data = json.loads(request.body)

        article.title = data['title']
```

```python
        article.content = data['content']

        article.publication_date =
data['publication_date']

        article.save()

        return JsonResponse({'id': article.id,
'title': article.title, 'content':
article.content, 'publication_date':
str(article.publication_date)})

    return JsonResponse({'error': 'Invalid
request method'}, status=400)


@csrf_exempt

def article_delete(request, pk):

    article = get_object_or_404(Article, pk=pk)

    if request.method == 'DELETE':

        article.delete()

        return JsonResponse({'message': 'Article
deleted'})

    return JsonResponse({'error': 'Invalid
request method'}, status=400)
```

This code provides the basic structure for handling CRUD operations on articles. You would then adapt it to your specific needs, such as adding authentication or more complex validation.

3. Generating Data Access Layers

If you're using a specific database library, like SQLAlchemy in Python, you can use AI to generate the code for interacting with your database tables.

You could provide a prompt like this:

"Generate SQLAlchemy code for interacting with a table named 'users' with columns 'id' (integer, primary key), 'name' (string), and 'age' (integer)."

The AI might generate code like this:

```python
Python

from sqlalchemy import create_engine, Column,
Integer, String

from sqlalchemy.ext.declarative import
declarative_base

from sqlalchemy.orm import sessionmaker


Base = declarative_base()


class User(Base):

    __tablename__ = 'users'


    id = Column(Integer, primary_key=True)

    name = Column(String)
```

```python
    age = Column(Integer)


    def __repr__(self):

        return f"<User(name='{self.name}',
age='{self.age}')>"


engine = create_engine('sqlite:///:memory:',
echo=True)

Base.metadata.create_all(engine)


Session = sessionmaker(bind=engine)

session = Session()


# Example usage:

# new_user = User(name='Alice', age=30)

# session.add(new_user)

# session.commit()
```

This generates the SQLAlchemy code for defining the table
structure and interacting with it. You can then use this code to
perform database operations in your application.

It's important to remember that while generative AI can be
incredibly helpful for generating boilerplate, it's not a replacement
for your understanding of the code. You still need to review the

generated code, ensure it meets your specific requirements, and integrate it correctly into your project. However, by offloading the tedious work of writing boilerplate, you can significantly increase your productivity and focus on the more interesting and valuable aspects of software development.

5.2 Automating Unit Test Creation

Let's talk about testing, specifically unit testing. We all know it's essential, right? It's the bedrock of reliable software. But let's be honest, writing unit tests can be a bit of a chore, especially for complex functions or classes. It's time-consuming, and sometimes it feels like we're just going through the motions.

This is another area where generative AI can significantly improve our workflow. It can help us automate the creation of unit tests, making the process faster, more efficient, and potentially more comprehensive.

Why is this so valuable? Unit tests are small, isolated tests that verify the behavior of individual units of code, like functions or methods.

They're crucial because they:

- Catch bugs early: They help us find errors in our code before they become bigger problems.
- Improve code quality: They force us to write cleaner, more modular code.
- Enable refactoring: They give us confidence to change our code, knowing that we can easily verify that we haven't broken anything.
- Document code: They provide a form of documentation, showing how the code is supposed to work.

However, writing effective unit tests requires careful consideration of various scenarios, including normal cases, edge cases, and error conditions. This can be time-consuming, and it's easy to miss some important test cases.

Generative AI can help us automate this process by analyzing our code and generating test cases that cover different aspects of its behavior. It can even suggest test cases that we might not have thought of ourselves.

Let's look at some examples:

1. Testing a Simple Function

Suppose we have a Python function that adds two numbers:

```python
Python

def add(a, b):

    """Adds two numbers."""

    return a + b
```

We can use generative AI to create a basic unit test for this function.

We could provide a prompt like this:

"Generate Python unit tests for the add function."

The AI might generate code like this:

```python
Python

import unittest


class TestAddFunction(unittest.TestCase):
```

```python
    def test_positive_numbers(self):

        self.assertEqual(add(2, 3), 5)


    def test_negative_numbers(self):

        self.assertEqual(add(-2, -3), -5)


    def test_mixed_numbers(self):

        self.assertEqual(add(2, -3), -1)


    def test_zero(self):

        self.assertEqual(add(0, 5), 5)


if __name__ == '__main__':

    unittest.main()
```

This generates a basic test suite that covers different input scenarios.

2. Testing a Function with Exceptions

Now, let's consider a function that raises an exception:

Python

```python
def divide(a, b):
```

```
"""Divides two numbers."""

if b == 0:

    raise ValueError("Cannot divide by zero")

return a / b
```

We can use generative AI to generate a unit test that verifies that the exception is raised correctly.

You could provide a prompt like this:

"Generate Python unit tests for the divide function, including a test case for the ValueError exception."

The AI might generate code like this:

```Python
import unittest


class TestDivideFunction(unittest.TestCase):


    def test_valid_division(self):

        self.assertEqual(divide(10, 2), 5.0)


    def test_division_by_zero(self):

        with self.assertRaises(ValueError):

            divide(10, 0)
```

```python
if __name__ == '__main__':

    unittest.main()
```

This test suite includes a test_division_by_zero method that uses self.assertRaises to assert that the ValueError exception is raised when we try to divide by zero.

3. Testing a Class Method

Let's consider an example with a class:

Python

```python
class Calculator:

    def add(self, a, b):

        return a + b


    def multiply(self, a, b):

        return a * b
```

We can use generative AI to generate unit tests for the methods of this class.

You could provide a prompt like this:

"Generate Python unit tests for the Calculator class, testing both the add and multiply methods."

The AI might generate code like this:

Python

```python
import unittest


class TestCalculator(unittest.TestCase):


    def setUp(self):

        self.calculator = Calculator()


    def test_add(self):

        self.assertEqual(self.calculator.add(2,
3), 5)


    def test_multiply(self):

self.assertEqual(self.calculator.multiply(2, 3),
6)


if __name__ == '__main__':

    unittest.main()
```

This test suite includes tests for both the add and multiply methods. It also uses the setUp method to create a Calculator object before each test.

It's important to note that while generative AI can be very helpful for automating unit test creation, it's not a replacement for our own understanding of testing principles. We still need to review the generated tests, ensure that they're comprehensive, and add any necessary test cases that the AI might have missed.

However, by leveraging AI to handle the more repetitive aspects of unit test creation, we can significantly speed up the testing process and improve the overall quality of our code. It's a powerful tool that can help us build more reliable and robust software.

5.3 Code Refactoring with AI

Alright, let's have a good chat about refactoring. If you're a coder, you've been there. It's the process of tidying up your code, making it cleaner, more organized, and easier to work with, all *without* changing what the code actually *does*. Think of it like reorganizing your workspace – you're not building anything new, but you're making it a much better place to work.

Why do we even bother with refactoring? Well, the benefits are pretty significant:

- Readability: Clean code is easier to understand, both for you and anyone else who has to work with it. This is huge for collaboration and long-term maintainability.
- Maintainability: When code is well-structured, it's much easier to modify, extend, and fix bugs. You spend less time wrestling with the code and more time adding features or solving problems.
- Complexity Reduction: Refactoring can simplify convoluted logic, making the code less prone to errors and easier to reason about.
- Performance: Sometimes, refactoring can reveal opportunities to optimize your code for speed or resource usage.

But here's the thing: refactoring can be tricky. It requires a solid grasp of the existing code, and you need to be careful not to introduce new bugs while you're making changes. It can also be time-consuming, especially in large and complex codebases.

This is where generative AI can step in as a valuable assistant. AI models can analyze code and suggest refactoring improvements, automating some of the more repetitive or pattern-based aspects of the process.

Let's look at some concrete examples of how AI can help:

1. Simplifying Conditional Logic

One common area where code can become complex is in conditional statements (if-else blocks). AI can often suggest ways to simplify these.

Consider this Python example:

Python

```python
def get_discount(customer_type, order_total):
    if customer_type == "premium":
        if order_total > 100:
            discount = 0.15
        else:
            discount = 0.1
    elif customer_type == "standard":
        if order_total > 50:
            discount = 0.05
```

```python
        else:

            discount = 0.02

    else:

        discount = 0.0

    return discount
```

This code has nested if statements, which can be a bit hard to follow. AI could suggest refactoring it using a more concise approach, such as a lookup table or a more direct calculation:

Python

```python
def get_discount(customer_type, order_total):

    discounts = {

        "premium": {50: 0.1, 100: 0.15},

        "standard": {50: 0.02, 100: 0.05},

    }

    discount = 0.0

    if customer_type in discounts:

        for threshold in
sorted(discounts[customer_type], reverse=True):

            if order_total > threshold:

                discount =
discounts[customer_type][threshold]

                break
```

```
    return discount
```

This version is arguably cleaner and easier to extend if you need to add more customer types or discount tiers.

2. Extracting Methods/Functions

When a function or method becomes long and does too much, it's good practice to break it down into smaller, more focused functions. AI can help identify chunks of code that would benefit from extraction.

For example, consider this Java method:

```
Java

public void processOrder(Order order) {

    double total = 0;

    for (OrderItem item : order.getItems()) {

        total += item.getPrice() *
item.getQuantity();

    }


    double discount = 0;

    if (order.getCustomer().isPremium()) {

        discount = 0.1;

    } else {

        discount = 0.05;

    }
```

```java
    double finalTotal = total * (1 - discount);


    // Save order to database

    // ...


    // Send confirmation email

    // ...

}
```

AI could suggest extracting the price calculation and discount calculation into separate methods:

Java

```java
private double calculateTotal(Order order) {

    double total = 0;

    for (OrderItem item : order.getItems()) {

        total += item.getPrice() *
item.getQuantity();

    }

    return total;

}


private double calculateDiscount(Customer
customer) {
```

```
    if (customer.isPremium()) {

        return 0.1;

    } else {

        return 0.05;

    }

}
```

```
public void processOrder(Order order) {

    double total = calculateTotal(order);

    double discount =
calculateDiscount(order.getCustomer());

    double finalTotal = total * (1 - discount);


    // Save order to database

    // ...


    // Send confirmation email

    // ...

}
```

This makes the processOrder method shorter, easier to read, and more focused.

3. Replacing Loops with Higher-Order Functions

In languages like Python, higher-order functions (like map, filter, and reduce) can often provide more concise and efficient ways to process collections of data than traditional for loops. AI can suggest these replacements.

For example:

```python
Python

# Original code:

results = []

for x in numbers:

    results.append(x * 2)



# AI suggestion:

results = list(map(lambda x: x * 2, numbers))
```

The map function applies a function to each element of a list, often leading to more readable code.

4. Improving Naming

Good naming is crucial for code clarity. AI can help identify variables, functions, or classes with poor or ambiguous names and suggest better alternatives.

For example:

```python
Python

# Original code:
```

```python
def proc(arr):

    res = []

    for i in arr:

        if i > 5:

            res.append(i + 1)

    return res



# AI suggestion:

def process_numbers(numbers):

    processed_numbers = []

    for number in numbers:

        if number > 5:

            processed_numbers.append(number + 1)

    return processed_numbers
```

The second version uses more descriptive names (process_numbers, numbers, processed_numbers, number), making the code easier to understand.

It's really important to stress that AI is a *tool* to assist with refactoring, not a magic wand.

You, as the developer, still need to:

- Understand the suggestions: Don't blindly accept AI's recommendations. Make sure you understand *why* the AI is suggesting a change and whether it's appropriate for your context.

- Test thoroughly: Refactoring can introduce subtle bugs, so thorough testing is essential after any refactoring.
- Maintain control: You're the ultimate decision-maker. Use AI to get ideas and suggestions, but always exercise your own judgment.

By embracing AI as a refactoring assistant, you can significantly improve your productivity and create cleaner, more maintainable, and higher-quality code.

5.4 Case Studies

Okay, let's move from the individual techniques to the bigger picture. How does generative AI really change how we work as developers? To illustrate this, let's explore some case studies. These aren't just abstract ideas; they're grounded in the realities of software development and show how AI can make a significant difference.

Case Study 1: Accelerating Web API Development

Consider a team building a complex web application. A core part of their work involves creating numerous API endpoints for different functionalities: user management, product catalogs, order processing, and so on. Traditionally, this process is quite repetitive. Developers have to write similar code for each endpoint:

- Handling HTTP requests (GET, POST, etc.)
- Parsing request data
- Validating input
- Interacting with the database
- Formatting responses

This is classic boilerplate, and it consumes a lot of development time.

Now, let's see how generative AI can streamline this. The team could use AI to generate the basic structure for each API endpoint.

For example, for a "users" endpoint, they might provide a prompt like this:

"Generate Flask (Python) API endpoints for creating, retrieving, updating, and deleting users. User data includes 'user_id' (integer), 'username' (string), and 'email' (string). Use Flask-RESTful for resource handling."

The AI could then generate code similar to this:

```python
Python

from flask import Flask

from flask_restful import reqparse, abort, Api,
Resource


app = Flask(__name__)

api = Api(app)


USERS = {

    '1': {'username': 'JohnDoe', 'email':
'john.doe@example.com'},

    '2': {'username': 'JaneSmith', 'email':
'jane.smith@example.com'}
```

```python
}


def abort_if_user_doesnt_exist(user_id):

    if user_id not in USERS:

        abort(404, message="User {} doesn't
exist".format(user_id))


parser = reqparse.RequestParser()

parser.add_argument('username')

parser.add_argument('email')


# User

class User(Resource):

    def get(self, user_id):

        abort_if_user_doesnt_exist(user_id)

        return USERS[user_id]


    def delete(self, user_id):

        abort_if_user_doesnt_exist(user_id)

        del USERS[user_id]

        return '', 204
```

```python
    def put(self, user_id):

        abort_if_user_doesnt_exist(user_id)

        args = parser.parse_args()

        user = {'username': args['username'],
'email': args['email']}

        USERS[user_id] = user

        return user, 201


# UserList

class UserList(Resource):

    def get(self):

        return USERS


    def post(self):

        args = parser.parse_args()

        user_id = str(int(max(USERS.keys())) + 1)
if USERS else '1'

        USERS[user_id] = {'username':
args['username'], 'email': args['email']}

        return USERS[user_id], 201
```

```
api.add_resource(UserList, '/users')

api.add_resource(User, '/users/<string:user_id>')


if __name__ == '__main__':

    app.run(debug=True)
```

This generates the basic structure for the CRUD operations. The developers would then need to fill in the specific database interactions, validation rules, and error handling.

By automating the generation of this boilerplate, the team can:

- Reduce development time: They spend less time on repetitive coding and more time on the API's core logic.
- Improve consistency: The generated code follows a consistent structure, making it easier to maintain.
- Focus on business logic: Developers can concentrate on the unique requirements of the application, rather than the plumbing.[1]

Case Study 2: Enhancing Data Analysis Workflows

In a data science context, generative AI can significantly boost productivity.[2]

Data scientists often need to write code for tasks like:

- Data loading and preprocessing
- Feature engineering
- Model training and evaluation
- Data visualization

Many of these tasks involve repetitive code patterns.

Let's say a data scientist is working on a project to predict customer churn. They might use AI to generate code for common data preprocessing steps.

For example, they could provide a prompt like this:

"Generate Python code using pandas to:

1. Load the CSV file 'customer_data.csv'.
2. Fill missing values in the 'age' column with the median age.
3. Encode the categorical column 'customer_segment' using one-hot encoding.
4. Scale the numerical columns 'age' and 'total_spending' using StandardScaler."

The AI could generate code like this:

```
Python

import pandas as pd

from sklearn.preprocessing import StandardScaler,
OneHotEncoder


def
preprocess_customer_data(filename='customer_data.
csv'):

    """

    Loads customer data, fills missing values,
encodes categorical features,

    and scales numerical features.
```

```python
    """

    try:

        df = pd.read_csv(filename)


        # Fill missing values in 'age'

        df['age'].fillna(df['age'].median(),
inplace=True)


        # One-hot encode 'customer_segment'

        encoder =
OneHotEncoder(handle_unknown='ignore',
sparse_output=False)

        encoded_segments =
encoder.fit_transform(df[['customer_segment']])

        df = pd.concat([df,
pd.DataFrame(encoded_segments,
columns=encoder.get_feature_names_out(['customer_
segment']))], axis=1)

        df.drop('customer_segment', axis=1,
inplace=True)


        # Scale numerical columns

        scaler = StandardScaler()
```

```
        df[['age', 'total_spending']] =
scaler.fit_transform(df[['age',
'total_spending']])


        return df


    except FileNotFoundError:

        return "Error: File not found"


# Example usage:

processed_data = preprocess_customer_data()

print(processed_data.head())
```

This code generates the pandas and scikit-learn code for the specified preprocessing steps. The data scientist can then focus on the more creative and analytical aspects of the project, such as choosing the right model and interpreting the results.

By using AI to automate these tasks, data scientists can:

- Accelerate experimentation: They can quickly try out different preprocessing techniques and model configurations.[3]
- Improve code quality: The generated code is often more consistent and less prone to errors.
- Enhance collaboration: AI can help standardize code across the team.[4]

Case Study 3: Automating Game Development Tasks

Game development involves a lot of coding, from character movement and AI behavior to animation and physics.[5] Many of these tasks involve repetitive code patterns.

For example, generating code for handling basic character movement in a 2D game can be automated.

A game developer might provide a prompt like this:

"Generate C# code for Unity to handle 2D character movement. The character should move horizontally and vertically using input from the arrow keys. Include code for basic collision detection with objects tagged as 'Wall'."

The AI can generate code similar to this:

```
C#

using UnityEngine;


public class CharacterMovement2D : MonoBehaviour

{

    public float moveSpeed = 5f; // Speed of
movement

    private Rigidbody2D rb;


    void Start()

    {
```

```csharp
        rb = GetComponent<Rigidbody2D>();

    }



    void FixedUpdate()

    {

        float moveX =
Input.GetAxisRaw("Horizontal");

        float moveY =
Input.GetAxisRaw("Vertical");



        Vector2 movement = new Vector2(moveX,
moveY).normalized * moveSpeed *
Time.fixedDeltaTime;

        rb.MovePosition(rb.position + movement);

    }



    void OnCollisionEnter2D(Collision2D
collision)

    {

        if
(collision.gameObject.CompareTag("Wall"))

        {
```

```
        rb.velocity = Vector2.zero; // Stop
movement on collision

        }

    }

}
```

This code generates the basic logic for character movement and collision detection. The game developer can then customize it to fit the specific needs of their game.

By automating such tasks, game developers can:

- Speed up prototyping: They can quickly create and test different game mechanics.
- Reduce development time: They spend less time writing repetitive code and more time on game design and gameplay.
- Experiment with more ideas: They can explore different game mechanics without being bogged down by coding.

These case studies show how generative AI can significantly streamline development workflows across different domains. It's not about replacing developers; it's about empowering them to be more productive, creative, and efficient.

Chapter 6: Building Next-Gen Applications

Generative AI isn't just about automating small tasks; it's about enabling us to create entirely new kinds of applications. This chapter explores some of the most promising areas where generative AI is poised to revolutionize software development.

6.1 AI-Powered Chatbots and Assistants

Let's talk about something that's becoming more and more integrated into our digital lives: chatbots and virtual assistants. But we're not just talking about the basic ones; we're talking about the next generation, those powered by generative AI. This is where things get really interesting.

Traditional chatbots often feel... well, robotic. They rely heavily on pre-programmed scripts and rules. If you ask them a question they haven't been specifically programmed to answer, they stumble. They struggle with nuance, with context, with the natural flow of human conversation.

Generative AI changes all that. It allows us to build chatbots and assistants that are far more sophisticated, capable of much more natural and engaging interactions.

At the heart of these advanced chatbots are large language models (LLMs). These models, as we discussed earlier, are trained on massive amounts of text data.

This training allows them to:

- Understand Natural Language: LLMs can process and interpret human language with a much greater degree of accuracy than traditional methods. They can handle variations in phrasing, understand context, and even grasp some level of sentiment. This means they can understand what you mean, not just what you say.

- Generate Human-Like Responses: LLMs can generate text that is coherent, grammatically correct, and contextually relevant. They can produce responses that sound remarkably human, making the conversation feel more natural and less like interacting with a machine.
- Adapt to Conversational Styles: Some LLMs can even adapt their tone and style to match the user's personality or the context of the conversation. This allows for more personalized and engaging interactions.

So, what does this mean for the kinds of applications we can build? The possibilities are quite broad:

- Enhanced Customer Support: AI-powered chatbots can provide instant and efficient customer support, answering questions, troubleshooting problems, and guiding users through processes. They can handle a large volume of inquiries simultaneously, freeing up human agents to focus on more complex issues.
- Personalized Recommendations: Chatbots can analyze user data and preferences to provide tailored recommendations for products, services, or content. This can improve user engagement and drive sales.
- Task Automation: Virtual assistants can automate tasks such as scheduling appointments, making reservations, placing orders, and providing reminders. This can save users time and effort.
- Improved Accessibility: AI-powered assistants can provide valuable support to users with disabilities, such as providing text-to-speech functionality or assisting with navigation.

Let's look at some examples to make this more concrete:

1. Building a Customer Support Chatbot

Imagine you're building a chatbot for an e-commerce website. You want it to be able to answer customer questions about products, orders, and shipping.

Here's how you might approach this using generative AI:

- Choose a Suitable LLM: You'd select a pre-trained LLM that has been fine-tuned for conversational tasks.
- Design the Conversation Flow: You'd define the basic structure of the conversation, including how the chatbot should greet users, handle common questions, and escalate to a human agent if necessary.
- Handle User Input: You'd write code to process the user's input, extract relevant information (e.g., keywords, intent), and format it as a prompt for the LLM.
- Generate a Response: You'd use the LLM to generate a response based on the user's input and the conversation context.
- Integrate with Other Systems: You'd connect the chatbot to your website's database to retrieve information about products, orders, and shipping.

Here's a simplified Python example of how you might use a pre-trained LLM (using the transformers library) to generate a response:

```
Python

import transformers


model_name = "microsoft/DialoGPT-medium"  #
Example model
```

```
tokenizer =
transformers.AutoTokenizer.from_pretrained(model_
name)

model =
transformers.AutoModelForCausalLM.from_pretrained
(model_name)


def generate_response(user_input, chat_history):

    new_input_ids = tokenizer.encode(user_input +
tokenizer.eos_token, return_tensors="pt")

    bot_input_ids = torch.cat([chat_history,
new_input_ids], dim=-1) if chat_history is not
None else new_input_ids


    chat_history = model.generate(

        bot_input_ids,

        max_length=1000,

        pad_token_id=tokenizer.eos_token_id,

        no_repeat_ngram_size=3,

        do_sample=True,

        top_p=0.7,

        top_k=50,

        temperature=0.7,
```

```
    )


    response = tokenizer.decode(chat_history[:,
bot_input_ids.shape[-1]:][0],
skip_special_tokens=True)

    return response, chat_history



# Example Usage

user_input = "What is the shipping cost?"

chat_history = None  # Initialize chat history

response, chat_history =
generate_response(user_input, chat_history)

print(f"Chatbot: {response}")



user_input = "Thanks!"

response, chat_history =
generate_response(user_input, chat_history)

print(f"Chatbot: {response}")
```

This is a simplified example, but it demonstrates the basic process of using an LLM to generate chatbot responses. In a real-world application, you'd need to add more sophisticated logic for managing the conversation flow, accessing external data, and handling errors.

2. Building a Personal Assistant

Another exciting application is building personal assistants that can help users with various tasks.

These assistants can:

- Schedule appointments
- Set reminders
- Provide information
- Control smart home devices

Generative AI can enable these assistants to understand complex commands and generate natural-sounding responses.

For example, you could build an assistant that can understand commands like:

- "Remind me to buy groceries at 6 PM today."
- "What's the weather forecast for tomorrow?"
- "Play some music."

The assistant would need to:

- Parse the user's command to understand the intent and extract relevant information (e.g., time, task, location).
- Use an LLM to generate a response that confirms the action or provides the requested information.
- Interact with external systems (e.g., calendar, weather API, music player) to fulfill the user's request.

Building these kinds of assistants is a complex undertaking, but generative AI makes it possible to create systems that are much more powerful and intuitive than previous generations.

It's important to remember that building AI-powered chatbots and assistants is an ongoing process. We need to continuously refine our models, improve our conversation designs, and address ethical considerations such as bias and privacy. However, the potential of these technologies to transform how we interact with computers is immense.

6.2 Domain-Specific Language Generation

Let's explore a really fascinating area where generative AI can make a big impact: the creation of domain-specific languages, or DSLs. This is a bit of a niche topic, but it has the potential to revolutionize how we interact with specialized systems and tools.

So, what exactly *is* a DSL? It's a computer language designed to be used within a particular field or "domain." Think of it as a mini-language tailored to a specific purpose.

Here are some examples to make this clearer:

- SQL (Structured Query Language): This is a DSL for interacting with databases. It's designed to express database queries and manipulations in a concise and declarative way.
- Regular Expressions: These are a DSL for defining search patterns in text. They're used in many programming languages and text editors.
- HTML (HyperText Markup Language): While not a programming language in the strictest sense, HTML is a DSL for structuring content on web pages.

The key thing about DSLs is that they're designed to be more expressive and easier to use than general-purpose programming languages (like Python or Java) *within their specific domain.* They allow domain experts (like financial analysts or biologists) to work more directly with systems without needing to become full-fledged programmers.

However, creating DSLs can be a complex and time-consuming process.

It involves:

- Defining the syntax: What keywords and grammar rules will the DSL use?
- Defining the semantics: What does each statement in the DSL *mean*?
- Building a parser: A program that can understand and interpret the DSL.
- Building tools: Editors, compilers, or interpreters for the DSL.

This is where generative AI can come in. AI models can automate many of these steps, making it much easier to create and use DSLs.

Here's how it works:

1. Prompt Engineering: We provide the AI model with a description of the domain and the tasks that the DSL should support.
2. Syntax and Semantics Generation: The AI model uses its understanding of language and code to generate the syntax and semantics of the DSL.
3. Parser Generation: The AI model can also generate code for a parser that can understand the DSL.
4. Tool Generation: In some cases, the AI can even assist in generating basic tools for the DSL, such as editors or interpreters.

Let's illustrate this with a simplified example. Suppose we want to create a DSL for describing simple geometric shapes.

We could provide the AI with a prompt like this:

"Generate a domain-specific language (DSL) for describing basic geometric shapes. The DSL should support the following shapes: circle, square, rectangle, triangle. It should allow specifying the dimensions of each shape (e.g., radius for a circle, side length for a square). It should also allow specifying the color of the shape. Generate a parser for this DSL in Python."

The AI might generate a DSL with syntax like this:

shape: <shape_type> <dimension_specifiers>
color=<color_name>

shape_type: circle | square | rectangle | triangle

dimension_specifiers:

  circle: radius=<number>

  square: side=<number>

  rectangle: width=<number> height=<number>

  triangle: base=<number> height=<number>

color_name: red | green | blue | ...

And it might generate a Python parser using a library like ply (Python Lex-Yacc):

```
Python

import ply.lex as lex

import ply.yacc as yacc


# --- Lexer ---
```

```python
tokens = ('SHAPE', 'CIRCLE', 'SQUARE',
'RECTANGLE', 'TRIANGLE',

          'RADIUS', 'SIDE', 'WIDTH', 'HEIGHT',
'BASE',

          'COLOR', 'EQUALS', 'NUMBER', 'NAME')


t_SHAPE = r'shape'

t_CIRCLE = r'circle'

t_SQUARE = r'square'

t_RECTANGLE = r'rectangle'

t_TRIANGLE = r'triangle'

t_RADIUS = r'radius'

t_SIDE = r'side'

t_WIDTH = r'width'

t_HEIGHT = r'height'

t_BASE = r'base'

t_COLOR = r'color'

t_EQUALS = r'='


t_NAME = r'[a-zA-Z_][a-zA-Z0-9_]*'
```

```python
def t_NUMBER(t):
    r'\d+'
    t.value = int(t.value)
    return t


t_ignore = ' \t'


def t_newline(t):
    r'\n+'
    t.lexer.lineno += len(t.value)


def t_error(t):
    print("Illegal character '%s'" % t.value[0])
    t.lexer.skip(1)


lexer = lex.lex()


# --- Parser ---
def p_shape(p):
    '''shape : SHAPE shape_type
dimension_specifiers COLOR EQUALS NAME'''
```

```python
    p[0] = {'type': p[2], 'dimensions': p[3],
'color': p[6]}


def p_shape_type(p):

    '''shape_type : CIRCLE | SQUARE | RECTANGLE |
TRIANGLE'''

    p[0] = p[1]


def p_dimension_specifiers(p):

    '''dimension_specifiers : circle_dimensions |
square_dimensions | rectangle_dimensions |
triangle_dimensions'''

    p[0] = p[1]


def p_circle_dimensions(p):

    '''circle_dimensions : RADIUS EQUALS
NUMBER'''

    p[0] = {'radius': p[3]}


def p_square_dimensions(p):

    '''square_dimensions : SIDE EQUALS NUMBER'''

    p[0] = {'side': p[3]}
```

```python
def p_rectangle_dimensions(p):

    '''rectangle_dimensions : WIDTH EQUALS NUMBER
HEIGHT EQUALS NUMBER'''

    p[0] = {'width': p[3], 'height': p[5]}


def p_triangle_dimensions(p):

    '''triangle_dimensions : BASE EQUALS NUMBER
HEIGHT EQUALS NUMBER'''

    p[0] = {'base': p[3], 'height': p[5]}


def p_error(p):

    if p:

        print("Syntax error at token", p.type)

    else:

        print("Syntax error at EOF")


parser = yacc.yacc()


# Example usage:

input_string = "shape circle radius=10 color=red"

result = parser.parse(input_string)
```

```
print(result)
```

This is a simplified example, but it demonstrates the potential of generative AI to automate the creation of DSLs.

The benefits of this are significant:

- Increased Productivity: Domain experts can work more efficiently by using DSLs tailored to their needs.
- Improved Communication: DSLs can provide a common language for communication between developers and domain experts.
- Reduced Complexity: DSLs can simplify complex tasks by providing a more intuitive and expressive way to interact with systems.

Generative AI can democratize DSL creation, making it accessible to a wider range of developers and domain experts. This can lead to the development of more powerful and user-friendly tools for various industries.

6.3 Automated API Generation

Alright, let's talk about something that's fundamental to modern software development: APIs. Application Programming Interfaces are the glue that allows different software systems to communicate with each other. They're essential for everything from web applications and mobile apps to microservices and cloud-based systems.

However, designing and building APIs can be a significant undertaking.

It involves:

- Defining endpoints: Specifying the URLs that clients can use to access different functionalities.

- Handling requests: Processing incoming requests from clients, parsing data, and validating input.
- Accessing data: Retrieving data from databases or other data sources.
- Generating responses: Formatting data into a suitable format (e.g., JSON, XML) and sending it back to the client.
- Authentication and authorization: Ensuring that only authorized clients can access the API.
- Documentation: Providing clear and accurate documentation for the API.

This process can be time-consuming and repetitive, especially when building APIs for a large number of resources or functionalities.

This is where generative AI can really shine. AI models can automate many aspects of API generation, significantly speeding up development and improving efficiency.

Here's how it works in principle:

1. API Specification: We provide the AI model with a specification of the API. This specification can be in various formats, such as:
    - Natural language descriptions: A textual description of the API's functionality.
    - API definition formats: Formats like OpenAPI Specification (formerly Swagger) or GraphQL schema.
    - Database schema: The structure of the underlying database.
2. Code Generation: The AI model uses the specification to generate the code for the API, including:
    - Endpoint definitions
    - Request handling logic
    - Data access code

- ○ Response formatting
- ○ (Sometimes) Basic authentication/authorization
3. Customization: The generated code can be further customized and refined by developers to meet specific requirements.

Let's look at some examples to illustrate this.

1. Generating a RESTful API from a Database Schema

Suppose you have a database table named "products" with columns like product_id (integer, primary key), name (string), description (text), and price (decimal). You want to create a RESTful API to access this data.

You could provide the AI model with the database schema (or a simplified representation of it):

Table: products

Columns:

   product_id: INTEGER, PRIMARY KEY

   name: VARCHAR(255)

   description: TEXT

   price: DECIMAL

The AI could then generate code for API endpoints like:
- GET /products: To retrieve a list of all products.
- GET /products/{product_id}: To retrieve a specific product by its ID.
- POST /products: To create a new product.
- PUT /products/{product_id}: To update an existing product.

- DELETE /products/{product_id}: To delete a product.

Here's a conceptual example of how this might look in Python using a framework like Flask (note that this is a simplified illustration and would require adaptation for a real-world database connection):

Python

```python
from flask import Flask, jsonify, request

from flask_restful import Api, Resource, reqparse


app = Flask(__name__)

api = Api(app)


# (In a real application, you'd connect to a
database here)

PRODUCTS = {}  # Placeholder for database data


class ProductList(Resource):

    def get(self):

        return jsonify(list(PRODUCTS.values()))


    def post(self):

        parser = reqparse.RequestParser()
```

```python
        parser.add_argument('name', type=str,
required=True)

        parser.add_argument('description',
type=str)

        parser.add_argument('price', type=float,
required=True)

        args = parser.parse_args()


        product_id = len(PRODUCTS) + 1   #
Simplified ID generation

        product = {

            'product_id': product_id,

            'name': args['name'],

            'description': args['description'],

            'price': args['price']

        }

        PRODUCTS[str(product_id)] = product

        return jsonify(product), 201


class Product(Resource):

    def get(self, product_id):

        if str(product_id) not in PRODUCTS:
```

```python
        return jsonify({'message': 'Product
not found'}), 404

        return jsonify(PRODUCTS[str(product_id)])


    def put(self, product_id):
        if str(product_id) not in PRODUCTS:
            return jsonify({'message': 'Product
not found'}), 404


        parser = reqparse.RequestParser()
        parser.add_argument('name', type=str)
        parser.add_argument('description',
type=str)
        parser.add_argument('price', type=float)
        args = parser.parse_args()


        product = PRODUCTS[str(product_id)]
        if args['name']: product['name'] =
args['name']
        if args['description']:
product['description'] = args['description']
        if args['price']: product['price'] =
args['price']
```

```python
        return jsonify(product)


    def delete(self, product_id):

        if str(product_id) not in PRODUCTS:

            return jsonify({'message': 'Product
not found'}), 404

        del PRODUCTS[str(product_id)]

        return '', 204


api.add_resource(ProductList, '/products')

api.add_resource(Product,
'/products/<int:product_id>')


if __name__ == '__main__':

    app.run(debug=True)
```

This code provides a basic RESTful API for interacting with products. The AI has generated the endpoints, request handling logic, and response formatting. A developer would then need to adapt this code to connect to their actual database and add more specific logic.

2. Generating GraphQL APIs

Generative AI can also assist in creating GraphQL APIs. You could provide the AI model with a GraphQL schema, and it could generate the code for resolvers (the functions that fetch data for GraphQL queries).

For example, given a GraphQL schema like this:

GraphQL

type Query {

   products: [Product]

   product(id: ID!): Product

}

type Mutation {

   createProduct(name: String!, description: String, price: Float!): Product

   updateProduct(id: ID!, name: String, description: String, price: Float): Product

   deleteProduct(id: ID!): Boolean

}

type Product {

   id: ID!

   name: String!

```
    description: String

    price: Float!

}
```

The AI could generate code for the resolvers in your chosen GraphQL server library (e.g., GraphQL-Python, Apollo Server).

3. Generating API Documentation

Beyond the code itself, generative AI can also help automate the creation of API documentation. By analyzing the API code or specification, the AI can generate documentation in formats like OpenAPI Specification or human-readable guides.

This can save developers a significant amount of time and ensure that the API is well-documented.

The benefits of automated API generation are substantial:

- Faster Development: Reduces the time and effort required to build APIs.
- Improved Consistency: Ensures that APIs follow consistent design principles and coding standards.
- Reduced Errors: Can help prevent common errors in API development.
- Increased Productivity: Frees up developers to focus on more complex and valuable tasks.

It's important to remember that AI is a tool to aid in API generation. Developers still need to review and customize the generated code, ensure it meets specific requirements, and handle complex logic that may not be easily automated. However, AI can significantly streamline the API development process, leading to faster and more efficient software development.

6.4 Automated Documentation

Let's talk about something that's both incredibly important and often sadly neglected in software development: documentation. We all know we *should* do it, but let's be honest, it often falls by the wayside when deadlines loom.

Documentation is the set of materials that describe how software works.

It's crucial for several reasons:

- Onboarding new developers: It helps new team members understand the codebase quickly.
- Maintenance: It makes it easier to modify and fix bugs in the code.
- Collaboration: It facilitates communication between developers working on different parts of the project.
- User support: It provides guidance to users on how to use the software.

However, writing documentation is often seen as a tedious and time-consuming task. It can be difficult to keep documentation up-to-date with code changes. And it can be challenging to create documentation that is both comprehensive and easy to understand.

This is where generative AI can be a game-changer. AI models can automate many aspects of documentation generation, making the process faster, more efficient, and more accurate.

Here's how AI can help:

1. Generating Documentation from Code

AI models can analyze code and automatically generate documentation, such as:

- API documentation: Generating descriptions of API endpoints, request/response formats, and authentication methods.
- Code comments: Adding comments to code to explain its functionality.
- Function/method documentation: Generating descriptions of function parameters, return values, and behavior.
- Class documentation: Creating documentation for classes, including their attributes and methods.

For example, consider this Python function:

Python

```python
def calculate_area(length, width):

    """

    Calculates the area of a rectangle.


    Args:

        length (float): The length of the
rectangle.

        width (float): The width of the
rectangle.


    Returns:

        float: The area of the rectangle.

    """
```

```
    return length * width
```

AI can analyze this code and generate documentation like this (in a different format, such as Markdown or HTML):

Function: calculate_area

Description:

Calculates the area of a rectangle.

Parameters:

`length` (float): The length of the rectangle.

`width` (float): The width of the rectangle.

Returns:

`float`: The area of the rectangle.

Example:

```python
calculate_area(5.0, 10.0)  # Returns 50.0
```

This can significantly reduce the effort required to document code.

2. Creating Tutorials and Guides

AI models can also generate tutorials and guides for using software. This can be helpful for both developers and end-users.

For example, you could provide the AI with a description of a software feature and ask it to generate a step-by-step tutorial on how to use it.

AI can even generate code examples to illustrate the usage of the feature.

3. Translating Documentation

AI can also be used to translate documentation into different languages. This can make software more accessible to a wider audience.

For example, you could provide the AI with documentation in English and ask it to translate it into Spanish, French, or Chinese.

4. Generating API Specifications

AI can assist in creating API specifications (e.g., OpenAPI Specification). You could provide the AI with a description of the API's functionality, and it could generate the corresponding specification file.

This can be very useful for automating the creation of API documentation and client libraries.

Let's look at a more detailed example. Suppose you have a Python class:

```python
class DataProcessor:
    """
```

A class for processing data.

"""

def __init__(self, data):

"""

Initializes the DataProcessor with input data.

Args:

data (list): The input data to process.

"""

self.data = data

def filter_data(self, threshold):

"""

Filters the data to include only values greater than
the threshold.

Args:

threshold (int): The threshold value.

Returns:

        list: A new list containing only the filtered values.

    """"""

    return [x for x in self.data if x > threshold]

    def calculate_average(self):

    """"""

        Calculates the average of the data.

        Returns:

            float: The average of the data.

    """"""

    if not self.data:

        return 0.0

    return sum(self.data) / len(self.data)

AI can analyze this class and generate comprehensive documentation, including:

- A class-level description.
- Descriptions of the __init__, filter_data, and calculate_average methods.
- Parameter and return value descriptions.
- Example usage.

This can significantly reduce the effort required to document classes and methods.

It's important to remember that while AI can automate much of the documentation process, human review is still essential. We need to ensure that the generated documentation is accurate, complete, and easy to understand.

However, by leveraging AI, we can make documentation a more integral part of the software development process, leading to better code quality, improved collaboration, and increased user satisfaction.

Chapter 7: Debugging and Code Optimization

This chapter explores how generative AI can assist us in finding and fixing bugs, as well as making our code run faster and more efficiently. We'll also discuss the limitations of AI-generated code and the importance of human oversight. Finally, we'll cover best practices to ensure that we're using AI responsibly and effectively in our debugging and optimization efforts.

7.1 Using AI for Bug Detection

Okay, let's face it: debugging is a fact of life for any coder. It's that process of hunting down and squashing those pesky errors (bugs) that prevent our code from working as intended. It can be time-consuming, frustrating, and sometimes feel like a detective novel where the culprit is always hiding.

But what if we had a more powerful detective on our side? That's where generative AI comes in. AI models are starting to show real potential in assisting with bug detection, and it's a development that could seriously change how we approach this crucial part of software development.

So, how can AI help us find those elusive bugs? It boils down to a few key capabilities:

- Pattern Recognition: AI models, especially those trained on vast amounts of code, can learn to recognize patterns associated with common errors. Think of it like a seasoned detective who's seen a lot of cases and knows the telltale signs of a crime.
- Static Analysis: This is a technique where the AI analyzes the code without actually running it. It's like examining a blueprint of a building to find structural weaknesses. AI can

use static analysis to identify potential issues like syntax errors, type errors, and some logical errors.

- Dynamic Analysis: This involves observing the code's behavior while it's running. It's like watching a building in use to see if it sways too much or if the plumbing leaks. AI can use dynamic analysis to detect runtime errors, memory leaks, and performance bottlenecks.

Let's break down these capabilities with some examples:

1. Spotting Syntax Errors

Syntax errors are the most basic type of error – they're like grammar mistakes in code. The code doesn't follow the rules of the programming language, and the computer can't even understand it.

AI can be very good at spotting these. For example, consider this Python code:

```
Python

def my_function(a, b)

    print(a + b)
```

The AI can quickly identify the missing colon after the function definition, which is a syntax error. It's like a spell checker for code.

2. Identifying Type Errors

Type errors occur when you try to perform an operation on data of the wrong type. For example, trying to add a number to a string.

AI can analyze the code and track the types of variables to find potential type errors.

For instance:

```
Python

def calculate_average(numbers):

    total = 0

    for num in numbers:

        total = total + num   # Potential
TypeError if numbers contains strings

    return total / len(numbers)
```

The AI can warn that if the numbers list contains strings, the + operator will cause a TypeError.

3. Detecting Logical Errors

Logical errors are where the code runs without crashing, but it doesn't do what you intended. These are often the hardest to find.

AI can sometimes help here by analyzing the flow of logic and identifying inconsistencies.

For example:

```
Python

def find_max(numbers):

    max_num = 0   # Incorrect initialization if
all numbers are negative

    for num in numbers:

        if num > max_num:
```

```
    max_num = num

  return max_num
```

The AI might point out that if the numbers list contains only negative numbers, the function will return 0, which is incorrect.

4. Finding Runtime Errors

Runtime errors occur while the program is running.

A common example is division by zero:

```
Python
```

```python
def divide(a, b):

    return a / b   # Potential ZeroDivisionError
if b is 0
```

AI can analyze the code and identify potential points where a ZeroDivisionError could occur.

5. Uncovering Security Vulnerabilities

This is a very important area.

AI can be trained to spot common security weaknesses in code, such as:

- SQL Injection: Vulnerabilities in database queries that allow attackers to inject malicious SQL code.
- Cross-Site Scripting (XSS): Vulnerabilities in web applications that allow attackers to inject malicious JavaScript code into web pages.

For example, consider this (simplified) PHP code:

```
PHP
```

```
$username = $_GET['username'];

$query = "SELECT * FROM users WHERE username =
'$username'";

// ... execute query ...
```

The AI can recognize that this code is vulnerable to SQL injection because the user-provided input $username is directly included in the SQL query without proper sanitization.

It's crucial to understand that while AI can be a powerful tool for bug detection, it's not foolproof. AI models learn from the data they're trained on, and they might not always catch every possible error. They can also sometimes generate "false positives," flagging code that is actually correct.

Therefore, human oversight is still essential. We should use AI as an *aid* in our debugging process, not as a complete replacement for our own skills and judgment.

Think of it like using a spell checker. It can catch many errors, but you still need to proofread your writing to ensure it's accurate and conveys the intended meaning.

By combining the power of AI with our own expertise, we can make debugging much more efficient and build more reliable software.

7.2 Code Improvement Suggestions

Okay, so AI isn't just about finding bugs; it can also be a pretty handy code reviewer, offering suggestions to make our code better. Think of it as having a very experienced, very patient colleague who's always there to point out ways to improve your code.

What kind of improvements are we talking about? Well, AI can help with several aspects of code quality:

- Readability: Making the code easier to understand for humans.
- Efficiency: Optimizing the code to run faster or use less memory.
- Style: Ensuring the code follows coding conventions and best practices.

Let's break these down with some examples:

1. Improving Readability

Readability is crucial. Code is read far more often than it's written, so making it easy to understand saves everyone time and reduces the risk of errors. AI can suggest ways to make code more readable, such as:

Replacing complex logic with simpler alternatives:

Consider this Python code:

```python
def get_status_message(status_code):
    if status_code == 200:
        message = "OK"
    elif status_code == 404:
        message = "Not Found"
    elif status_code == 500:
        message = "Internal Server Error"
```

```python
    else:
        message = "Unknown Status"
    return message
```
` ` `

AI might suggest using a dictionary for a more concise and readable approach:

` ` `python

```python
def get_status_message(status_code):
    status_messages = {
        200: "OK",
        404: "Not Found",
        500: "Internal Server Error"
    }
    return status_messages.get(status_code,
"Unknown Status")
```
` ` `

The dictionary version is often easier to grasp at a glance.

* **Suggesting better naming:**

Variable and function names should be descriptive. AI can point out names that are too short, cryptic, or misleading.

```python
# Original:

def proc(arr):
    res = []
    for i in arr:
        if i > 10:
            res.append(i * 2)
    return res


# AI suggestion:

def process_numbers(numbers):
    processed_numbers = []
    for number in numbers:
        if number > 10:
            processed_numbers.append(number * 2)
    return processed_numbers
```

The second version is much clearer about what the function does and what the variables represent.

2. Enhancing Efficiency

AI can also help us write code that runs more efficiently. This often involves:

Replacing inefficient loops:

In Python, `for` loops can sometimes be slow. AI might suggest using list comprehensions or the `map` function, which are often faster.

```python
# Original:

squared_numbers = []

for num in numbers:

    squared_numbers.append(num ** 2)



# AI suggestion:

squared_numbers = [num ** 2 for num in numbers]
```

List comprehensions are generally more efficient.

Optimizing data structures:

AI can suggest using the most appropriate data structure for a given task. For example, using a `set` for fast membership testing.

```python

# Original:

def contains_element(my_list, element):

    return element in my_list



# AI suggestion:

def contains_element(my_set, element):

    return element in my_set  # Sets offer faster
lookups

```

3. Enforcing Code Style

Code style is about consistency in formatting, indentation, naming conventions, and other code layout aspects. Consistent style makes code easier to read and maintain, especially in team projects.

AI can be trained to recognize and enforce various coding styles (e.g., PEP 8 for Python, Google Style Guide). It can automatically format code, suggest naming conventions, and point out style violations.

For example, AI might suggest:

Using consistent indentation (e.g., 4 spaces in Python).

Adding or removing whitespace to improve readability.

Recommending a specific naming convention (e.g., `camelCase` vs. `snake_case`).

It's important to remember that AI's suggestions are just that – suggestions. As developers, we still have the final say. We need to:

Understand the rationale: Don't blindly accept AI's recommendations. Make sure you understand *why* the AI is suggesting a change.

Consider context: The "best" code is often context-dependent. What's readable or efficient in one situation might not be in another.

Test thoroughly: Any code change, even a "small" refactoring, should be tested to ensure it doesn't introduce bugs.

By combining AI's analytical capabilities with our human judgment, we can write code that is not only functional but also clean, efficient, and maintainable. It's about using AI to elevate our coding craft.

7.3 Limitations of AI-Generated Code

Okay, it's really important to have a balanced perspective here. We've been talking about the amazing things AI can do for coding, but we also need to be realistic about its limitations. AI-generated code isn't perfect, and it's crucial to understand where it can fall short. It's like any tool – powerful, but you need to know its weaknesses to use it effectively.

The core issue stems from how AI models learn. They're trained on massive datasets, and they learn patterns and statistical relationships within that data. They don't have true understanding or common sense like humans do.

This leads to some key limitations:

1. Hallucinations (Incorrect Code)

AI models can sometimes generate code that looks correct but is actually wrong. This is often referred to as "hallucination," borrowing a term from language models that generate nonsensical text. In code, this means the AI produces code that has the correct syntax (it's valid code) but the wrong semantics (it doesn't do what you intended).

For example, you might ask the AI to generate a function to sort a list in descending order, and it might generate code that sorts it in ascending order instead.

Python

```
# Prompt: Generate a Python function to sort a
list in descending order.
```

```
# AI-generated code (incorrect):

def sort_descending(my_list):

    return sorted(my_list)  # Incorrect: sorts in
ascending order
```

```
# Correct code:

def sort_descending(my_list):

    return sorted(my_list, reverse=True)
```

The AI generated syntactically correct Python code, but it used the sorted() function without the reverse=True argument, resulting in ascending order sorting.

2. Bias and Fairness

AI models learn from their training data, and if that data contains biases, the generated code can also perpetuate those biases. This is a serious concern, especially when AI is used to generate code that makes decisions that affect people's lives (e.g., in loan applications or hiring systems).

For example, if the training data for an AI model that generates code for a loan application system contains historical data where certain demographic groups were unfairly disadvantaged, the AI might generate code that continues to perpetuate that bias.

3. Security Vulnerabilities

AI models might generate code that has security vulnerabilities, such as:

SQL Injection: Vulnerabilities in database queries that allow attackers to execute arbitrary SQL code.

Cross-Site Scripting (XSS): Vulnerabilities in web applications that allow attackers to inject malicious JavaScript code into web pages.

Consider this (simplified) JavaScript code generated by AI:

JavaScript

```
// Prompt: Generate JavaScript code to display a
user's name on a web page.

function displayUserName(username) {
```

```
document.getElementById('user-greeting').innerHTM
L = "Hello, " + username;

}
```

An AI might generate this code, but it's vulnerable to XSS. If username contains malicious JavaScript code, it will be executed when the page is displayed.

4. Lack of Context and Understanding

AI models don't have a true understanding of the overall context of a project or the specific business requirements. They generate code based on the prompt they receive and the patterns they've learned from the training data. This can lead to code that is:

Suboptimal: It might not be the most efficient or elegant solution.

Inappropriate: It might not be the best fit for the specific situation.

Incomplete: It might require significant manual modification to integrate into the existing codebase.

For example, you might ask the AI to generate code for handling user authentication, and it might generate a basic implementation that doesn't consider important security best practices.

5. Copyright and Licensing Issues

AI models are trained on existing code, which is often subject to copyright and licensing restrictions. There are ongoing legal and ethical debates about whether AI-generated code infringes on these rights.

It's important to be aware of these issues and to use AI-generated code responsibly.

What Does This Mean for Us?

It means we can't blindly trust AI-generated code. We need to treat it as a tool, a powerful tool, but one that requires careful human oversight.

We need to:

Review the code: Always carefully examine the generated code to ensure it's correct, efficient, and secure.

Test rigorously: Thoroughly test the code to catch any errors or unexpected behavior.

Understand the limitations: Be aware of the potential limitations of AI-generated code and take steps to mitigate them.

Think of it like using a compiler. A compiler can translate your code into machine code, but you still need to write the code correctly in the first place. AI is a powerful tool, but it's not a replacement for our skills and judgment as developers.

7.4 Best Practices for Debugging and Optimization

Okay, so we've explored how AI can help with debugging and optimization, but we've also acknowledged its limitations. Now, let's talk about how to use AI effectively and responsibly in these areas. It's about combining the power of AI with our own skills and expertise to create the best possible outcome.

Here are some key best practices:

1. Human Oversight: Always Review and Test

This is absolutely crucial. Never treat AI-generated code as a "black box" that you can blindly trust. Always carefully review and test the code.

- Code Review: Treat AI-generated code like code written by a junior developer. Examine it line by line. Look for:
    - Logical errors: Does it do what you intend?
    - Efficiency: Is it the most efficient way to achieve the result?
    - Security vulnerabilities: Is it susceptible to attacks?
    - Style: Does it follow your project's coding conventions?
- Thorough Testing: Write unit tests, integration tests, and perform manual testing to ensure the code behaves as expected in different scenarios. Pay special attention to edge cases and error conditions.

For example, if AI suggests a code optimization, don't just assume it's correct. Benchmark the code before and after the change to verify that it actually improves performance.

2. Understand the Suggestions

Don't just blindly accept AI's recommendations. Try to understand why the AI is suggesting a particular change.

- Ask "Why?": If the AI suggests refactoring a piece of code, try to understand the reasoning behind the suggestion. Is it for readability? Efficiency? Maintainability?
- Learn from the AI: Use the AI's suggestions as an opportunity to learn new coding techniques or best practices.

- Reject inappropriate suggestions: If you disagree with the AI's suggestion, don't hesitate to reject it. You are the final decision-maker.

For instance, if AI suggests replacing a for loop with a list comprehension in Python, make sure you understand how list comprehensions work and whether they are indeed the best choice in that specific context.

3. Use AI as a Tool, Not a Replacement

Think of AI as a powerful assistant that can help you with certain tasks, but not as a substitute for your own skills and judgment.

- Focus on higher-level tasks: Use AI to handle the more repetitive or mechanical aspects of debugging and optimization, freeing you up to focus on more complex and creative tasks.
- Leverage your domain expertise: AI might not have the same understanding of your specific domain or business requirements as you do. Use your expertise to guide the AI and evaluate its suggestions.
- Maintain control: Remember that you are ultimately responsible for the quality and correctness of the code.

For example, if you're working on a performance-critical application, you might use AI to identify potential bottlenecks, but you would still need to use your knowledge of algorithms and data structures to implement the most effective optimizations.

4. Provide Clear and Specific Prompts

The quality of the AI's output depends heavily on the quality of your input.

When using AI for debugging and optimization, provide clear and specific prompts

- Be precise: Clearly describe the problem you're trying to solve or the code you want to improve.
- Give context: Provide the AI with relevant information about the code, such as its purpose, its inputs and outputs, and any constraints or requirements.
- Use examples: If possible, provide examples of the desired output or behavior.

For example, instead of asking the AI to "optimize this code," ask it to "identify potential performance bottlenecks in this Python function and suggest ways to improve its speed."

5. Embrace an Iterative Process

Debugging and optimization are often iterative processes. You make a change, test it, and then refine your approach based on the results.

Use AI to accelerate this process

- Generate and Test: Use AI to generate code or suggestions, and then test them thoroughly.
- Get Feedback: Analyze the results of your tests and use them to refine your prompts and guide the AI.
- Repeat: Continue iterating until you achieve the desired outcome.

For instance, you might use AI to generate several different versions of a function, test their performance, and then choose the best-performing version.

By following these best practices, you can effectively harness the power of AI to improve your debugging and optimization workflows, creating better, more efficient, and more reliable software.

Chapter 8: Fine-tuning and Customization

This chapter covers the techniques for adapting pre-trained generative AI models to specific tasks and datasets. We'll discuss the process of fine-tuning, the benefits of training on custom data, and, importantly, the ethical implications we need to be aware of when customizing AI.

8.1 Fine-tuning Pre-trained Models

Alright, let's talk about fine-tuning. Think of it as taking a really smart student and giving them some extra, specialized training to make them an expert in a particular subject. That's essentially what we're doing with pre-trained AI models.

We start with a model that's already learned a lot from a huge amount of data. It has a good general understanding of language, code, or whatever it was trained on. This is the "pre-trained" part. It's like having a student who's completed a general education.

But sometimes, we want that model to be really good at a very specific task. That's where fine-tuning comes in. We take that pre-trained model and train it *further* on a much smaller, more focused dataset. This dataset is tailored to the specific task we want the model to excel at.

Why would we do this? There are several compelling reasons:

- Improved Accuracy: Fine-tuning can dramatically increase the model's accuracy on the specific task. A language model might be decent at generating text in general, but fine-tuning it on a dataset of technical documentation will make it *much* better at generating accurate and concise technical descriptions.

- Efficiency: Fine-tuning is far more efficient than training a model from scratch. Training a large language model from the ground up requires massive amounts of data, computational power, and time. Fine-tuning, on the other hand, requires much less of all three. It's like giving that student a focused study guide instead of making them read every book in the library.
- Adaptation to Specific Styles or Conventions: Fine-tuning allows us to adapt the model to specific styles, formats, or conventions. For example, if you want a model to generate code in a particular coding style, you can fine-tune it on a dataset of code that adheres to that style.

So, how does fine-tuning actually work? The basic process involves these steps:

1. Select a Pre-trained Model: You begin with a model that's already been trained on a large and diverse dataset. This model provides a strong foundation of general knowledge.
2. Prepare a Specific Dataset: You create a smaller dataset that's highly relevant to the task you want the model to perform. The quality and relevance of this dataset are crucial.
3. Continue Training: You resume the training process, but this time, you only train the model on your specific dataset. The model adjusts its internal parameters to better perform the targeted task.

To give you a clearer picture, let's consider a simplified Python example using the transformers library, which is a popular tool for working with transformer models:

Python

```
import transformers
```

```python
import torch


# 1. Select a Pre-trained Model

model_name = "Salesforce/codegen-350M-multi"   #
Example model for code generation

tokenizer =
transformers.AutoTokenizer.from_pretrained(model_
name)

model =
transformers.AutoModelForCausalLM.from_pretrained
(model_name)


# 2. Prepare a Specific Dataset (Simplified
example)

# In reality, this would be a much larger dataset
of code examples

train_dataset = [

    "# Python function to calculate the area of a
rectangle",

    "def rectangle_area(length, width):\n
return length * width",

    "# Python function to find the maximum
element in a list",

    "def find_max(my_list):\n    return
max(my_list)"
```

```
]


# 3. Continue Training (Simplified example)

# We're using a simplified training loop for
demonstration

optimizer = torch.optim.AdamW(model.parameters(),
lr=5e-5)  # Optimizer for training

model.train()  # Put the model in training mode



for epoch in range(3):  # Number of training
iterations (epochs)

    for batch in train_dataset:

        inputs = tokenizer.encode(batch,
return_tensors="pt")  # Convert text to numerical
input

        outputs = model(inputs, labels=inputs)  #
Model's prediction and loss calculation

        loss = outputs.loss  # Calculate the loss
(error)

        loss.backward()  # Calculate gradients
(how to adjust model parameters)

        optimizer.step()  # Update model
parameters

        optimizer.zero_grad()  # Reset gradients
for the next iteration
```

```
model.eval()  # Put the model back in evaluation
mode
```

```
# Now the model is fine-tuned for generating
simple Python functions
```

```
# You could then use it to generate code based on
prompts
```

In this example:

- We start with a pre-trained code generation model (Salesforce/codegen-350M-multi).
- We create a small train_dataset with Python function examples.
- We use an optimizer to adjust the model's parameters based on the difference between its predictions and the actual code (the "loss").

It's crucial to remember that this is a simplified illustration.

In a real-world fine-tuning scenario, you'd deal with:

- Much larger datasets: You'd need a substantial amount of data to fine-tune effectively.
- More complex training loops: You'd need to handle batching, validation, and other training details.
- Hyperparameter tuning: You'd need to experiment with different training settings (learning rate, batch size, etc.) to optimize performance.

Fine-tuning is a powerful technique that allows us to adapt pre-trained AI models to a wide range of specific tasks. It's a key tool for building specialized and highly effective AI applications.

8.2 Training Models on Custom Datasets

Okay, so we've discussed fine-tuning, which is like giving a pre-trained model a focused education. But what if the subject you want to teach doesn't exist in any of the textbooks the model has already read? That's where training models on custom datasets comes into play. It's like building a student's knowledge from the ground up, tailored precisely to your needs.

Essentially, instead of starting with a model that already has a broad understanding, we start with a model that has *no* prior knowledge. We then feed it a dataset that we've created ourselves, teaching it from scratch.

Why go to all this trouble? There are some very good reasons:

- Highly Specialized Domains: Sometimes, you're working in a field where there are no readily available pre-trained models. Think about generating code for a very specific piece of hardware or software that uses a proprietary language. In these cases, you *have* to train on your own data.
- Granular Control: Training from scratch gives you maximum control over the model's behavior. You can shape it to generate code or text that perfectly matches your desired style, format, or conventions. This is important for applications where consistency is paramount.
- Data Privacy and Security: If you're dealing with sensitive data that you can't share with a third-party API or cloud service, training on your own infrastructure becomes essential. This ensures that your data stays within your control.

However, training a model from scratch is a significantly more involved process than fine-tuning.

It requires:

- A Substantial Dataset: To train a model effectively, you need a large and diverse dataset that covers the full range of inputs and outputs you expect the model to handle. The more complex the task, the more data you'll need.
- Computational Resources: Training large models demands significant computational power. You'll likely need access to powerful GPUs (Graphics Processing Units) or TPUs (Tensor Processing Units) to accelerate the training process.
- Machine Learning Expertise: Training from scratch involves making many design choices and tuning hyperparameters (settings that control the training process). This often requires a deeper understanding of machine learning principles.

Let's break down the key steps involved in training a model on a custom dataset

1. Dataset Creation: This is arguably the most crucial step. You need to gather or create a dataset that accurately represents the task you want the model to learn. This might involve collecting code samples, text documents, or any other relevant data.
    - For example, if you're training a model to generate code for a specific game engine, you'd need a dataset of code snippets written for that engine.
    - If you're training a model to generate product descriptions in a particular style, you'd need a dataset of existing product descriptions that match that style.
2. Data Preprocessing: Once you have your dataset, you'll need to clean and prepare it for training. This might involve:

- Tokenization: Breaking down text or code into smaller units (tokens).
- Data cleaning: Removing irrelevant or noisy data.
- Formatting: Ensuring the data is in a consistent format.

3. Model Architecture Selection: You need to choose the right neural network architecture for your task. For language-based tasks (like code generation), transformer architectures are often a good choice.

4. Training Loop Implementation: This is the core of the training process. You'll need to write code that:
   - Feeds data to the model in batches.
   - Calculates the model's predictions.
   - Measures the error between the predictions and the actual values (using a loss function).
   - Adjusts the model's parameters to reduce the error (using an optimizer).

5. Hyperparameter Tuning: You'll need to experiment with different hyperparameters to find the settings that give you the best performance. This is often an iterative process.

Let's look at a simplified conceptual example using Python and the torch library:

Python

```python
import torch

import torch.nn as nn

import torch.optim as optim

from torch.utils.data import DataLoader, Dataset
```

```python
# 1. Dataset Creation (Simplified example)

class MyDataset(Dataset):

    def __init__(self, data):

        self.data = data


    def __len__(self):

        return len(self.data)


    def __getitem__(self, idx):

        return self.data[idx]


data = [

    "def add(a, b): return a + b",

    "def subtract(a, b): return a - b",

    "def multiply(a, b): return a * b"

]

dataset = MyDataset(data)

dataloader = DataLoader(dataset, batch_size=2)   # Load data in batches
```

```python
# 2. Data Preprocessing (Simplified example - no
tokenization here)

# In reality, you'd need proper tokenization



# 3. Model Architecture Selection (Simplified
example - a basic RNN)

class MyModel(nn.Module):

    def __init__(self, input_size, hidden_size,
output_size):

        super().__init__()

        self.rnn = nn.RNN(input_size,
hidden_size, batch_first=True)

        self.fc = nn.Linear(hidden_size,
output_size)


    def forward(self, x):

        out, _ = self.rnn(x)

        out = self.fc(out[:, -1, :])   # Take the
last output

        return out



input_size = 10  # Simplified input size (e.g.,
embedding dimension)
```

```python
hidden_size = 32

output_size = 10   # Simplified output size (e.g.,
vocabulary size)

model = MyModel(input_size, hidden_size,
output_size)


# 4. Training Loop Implementation (Simplified
example)

criterion = nn.CrossEntropyLoss()   # Loss
function

optimizer = optim.Adam(model.parameters(),
lr=0.001)   # Optimizer


for epoch in range(5):   # Number of training
epochs

    for batch in dataloader:

        # (In reality, you'd need to convert the
text to numerical input here)

        inputs = torch.randn(2, 10, 10)   #
Simplified random input

        targets = torch.randint(0, 10, (2, 10))
# Simplified random targets


        outputs = model(inputs)
```

```
    loss = criterion(outputs, targets)


    optimizer.zero_grad()

    loss.backward()

    optimizer.step()


    print(f"Epoch {epoch+1}, Loss:
{loss.item()}")



# 5. Hyperparameter Tuning (Not shown - would
involve experimentation)



print("Training finished!")
```

This is a heavily simplified example to illustrate the core concepts.

In a real-world scenario, you'd deal with:

- Much larger datasets and models
- More sophisticated model architectures (like transformers)
- Proper tokenization and data encoding
- More complex training loops and loss functions
- Extensive hyperparameter tuning

Training models on custom datasets is a powerful technique, but it requires significant expertise and resources. It's often reserved for situations where fine-tuning isn't sufficient or where you need maximum control over the model's behavior.

8.3 Ethical Considerations in Fine-tuning

Okay, this is a really important area. We've been talking about the power of fine-tuning, how it lets us adapt AI models to do exactly what we want. But with that power comes a lot of responsibility. We need to think carefully about the ethical implications of what we're doing.

Fine-tuning, in particular, can amplify existing problems or introduce new ones if we're not careful. It's like giving someone a microphone; you want to make sure they're going to use it responsibly.

Here are some of the key ethical considerations we need to keep in mind:

1. Bias Amplification

AI models learn from the data they're trained on. If that data contains biases, the model will likely learn those biases too. And fine-tuning can actually amplify these biases.

Let's say you're fine-tuning a code generation model. If your fine-tuning dataset happens to contain a disproportionate amount of code written by one gender or demographic group, the model might start generating code that reflects the style or preferences of that group. This isn't inherently bad, but it can become problematic if it leads to the model excluding or misrepresenting other groups.

A more subtle example could be fine-tuning a model to generate documentation. If the training data contains documentation that uses gendered pronouns in a stereotypical way (e.g., always referring to engineers as "he"), the fine-tuned model might perpetuate those stereotypes.

It's crucial to be aware of the potential for bias and to take steps to mitigate it.

This means:

- Carefully Curating Datasets: Make sure your fine-tuning datasets are diverse and representative. Actively look for and correct any imbalances or stereotypes.
- Evaluating Models for Bias: Develop methods to assess the model's output for bias. This might involve analyzing the language it uses, the code it generates, or the decisions it makes.
- Employing Debiasing Techniques: There are various techniques you can use to reduce bias in AI models, such as data augmentation, adversarial training, and fairness constraints.

2. Misinformation and Manipulation

Fine-tuned language models can be incredibly good at generating realistic text. This raises concerns about their potential to be used to spread misinformation or manipulate people's opinions.

For example, imagine fine-tuning a language model on a dataset of political speeches. The model could then be used to generate highly convincing but completely fabricated speeches. This could have serious consequences in elections or public debates.

Similarly, fine-tuned chatbots could be used to impersonate individuals or organizations, spreading false information or engaging in deceptive practices.

To address these concerns, we need to:

- Develop Detection Methods: Research ways to detect AI-generated text and identify instances of misinformation.

- Promote Media Literacy: Educate the public about the potential for AI-generated misinformation and how to critically evaluate information.
- Establish Ethical Guidelines: Set clear ethical guidelines for the development and deployment of AI models, emphasizing responsible use and transparency.

3. Privacy Violations

Fine-tuning datasets can sometimes contain sensitive personal information. If the model learns to reproduce or reveal this information, it can lead to privacy violations.

For example, imagine fine-tuning a model on a dataset of customer service transcripts. These transcripts might contain customers' names, addresses, phone numbers, or other personal details. If the model generates responses that include this information, it could breach customer privacy.

To protect privacy, we need to:

- Anonymize Datasets: Remove or obscure any personally identifiable information from the fine-tuning dataset.
- Use Privacy-Preserving Techniques: Explore techniques like differential privacy, which can help prevent models from memorizing and revealing sensitive information.
- Establish Data Governance Policies: Implement strong data governance policies to ensure that data is collected, stored, and used ethically and responsibly.

4. Intellectual Property Issues

Fine-tuning a model on copyrighted material raises complex legal and ethical questions about intellectual property.

For example, if you fine-tune a model on a dataset of copyrighted code, does the generated code infringe on the copyright of the original code? This is a subject of ongoing debate and legal uncertainty.

To navigate these issues, we need to:

- Understand Copyright Law: Familiarize ourselves with the relevant copyright laws and regulations.
- Use Publicly Available Datasets: Prioritize the use of publicly available and permissively licensed datasets whenever possible.
- Seek Legal Counsel: If you're unsure about the legal implications of fine-tuning on specific datasets, seek legal counsel.

In essence, fine-tuning is a powerful tool, but it's not without its risks. We need to approach it with a strong sense of ethical responsibility, carefully considering the potential consequences of our actions. It's about using this technology to build a better future, not one that's riddled with bias, misinformation, or privacy violations.

Chapter 9: AI-Driven Software Architecture

This chapter explores how generative AI can be applied to the design and creation of software architectures. We'll discuss how AI can assist in the design process, automate the creation of scalable systems, and consider the future implications of this technology.

9.1 Designing Architectures with Generative AI

Alright, let's talk about something that's really at the forefront of software development: using generative AI to help us design software architectures. This is a big step beyond just generating code snippets; we're talking about AI assisting with the very blueprint of our applications.

So, what is software architecture anyway? It's the high-level structure of a software system. It defines the components, how they're organized, and how they interact with each other. Think of it like the architectural plans for a building. You wouldn't just start laying bricks without a plan, right? The same is true for software.

A well-designed architecture is absolutely crucial for a successful software project.

It determines:

- Maintainability: How easily can we change or update the system in the future?
- Scalability: Can the system handle increasing amounts of data or traffic?
- Reliability: Is the system stable and dependable? Does it handle errors gracefully?
- Security: Does the system protect sensitive data and prevent unauthorized access?

Traditionally, designing software architecture is a complex and time-consuming task. It requires a lot of experience and expertise.

Architects need to consider a wide range of factors, including:

- Functional requirements: What the system needs to *do*.
- Non-functional requirements: Things like performance, security, and scalability.
- Technology constraints: The tools and platforms we have available.
- Team capabilities: The skills and experience of the development team.

It's a bit like being a city planner, figuring out how all the roads, buildings, and utilities should fit together to create a functional and livable city.

Now, how can generative AI help with this? Well, AI models can be trained on a massive amount of data about software architectures, including:

- Architectural patterns (like microservices or message queues)
- Design principles (like separation of concerns)
- Code examples from successful and unsuccessful projects

This allows them to learn what works well and what doesn't.

Here are some ways AI can assist in the architecture design process:

- Suggesting Architectural Patterns: AI can analyze the requirements of a system and suggest appropriate architectural patterns.

    For example, if you tell the AI that you're building a system that needs to handle a high volume of concurrent users, it might suggest a microservices architecture with load balancing.

Or, if you tell the AI that you need a system that processes a large amount of data asynchronously, it might suggest using a message queue.

- Generating Architectural Diagrams: AI can create visual representations of the architecture, such as:
    - Component diagrams: Showing the different components of the system and their relationships.
    - Deployment diagrams: Showing how the system will be deployed on servers.
    - Sequence diagrams: Showing the interactions between different components over time.

This can help developers visualize the architecture and understand how the system works.

- Automating Code Generation: In some cases, AI can even generate code for the different components of the system, based on the architectural design.

For example, if you use a microservices architecture, the AI could generate the basic code for each service, including the API endpoints and the communication logic.

Let's walk through a more concrete example. Suppose you're building an e-commerce system.

You could provide the AI with a description of the system's requirements:

"Design an e-commerce system that supports:

User registration and authentication

Product browsing and searching

Shopping cart management

Order placement and tracking

Payment processing

The system should be scalable to handle a high volume of users and transactions. It should also be highly available, meaning it should be able to continue functioning even if some components fail."

The AI might then generate:

- A component diagram showing services like:
  - UserService: Handles user registration, authentication, and profile management.
  - ProductService: Manages the product catalog, including browsing and searching.
  - OrderService: Handles order creation, modification, and tracking.
  - PaymentService: Processes payments.
  - CartService: Manages user shopping carts.
- A description of the communication protocols between these services. For example:
  - UserService communicates with OrderService to retrieve user order history.
  - OrderService communicates with PaymentService to process payments.
- Basic code snippets for each service, such as:

- API endpoints for creating, retrieving, updating, and deleting users in UserService.
- Functions for adding items to the cart and calculating the cart total in CartService.

It's crucial to emphasize that AI is not intended to *replace* human architects. It's a tool to *assist* them. The AI's suggestions should be reviewed and refined by experienced professionals.

Human architects bring crucial skills that AI currently lacks:

- Creativity: The ability to come up with novel and innovative solutions.
- Intuition: The ability to make sound judgments based on experience and incomplete information.
- Ethical considerations: The ability to understand the social and ethical implications of architectural decisions.

AI can handle the more routine and computationally intensive aspects of architecture design, freeing up human architects to focus on the more creative, strategic, and ethical considerations.

In essence, AI-driven architecture is about combining the power of AI with the expertise of human architects to build better software systems, faster and more efficiently. It's a very exciting area with a lot of potential.

9.2 Automating Scalable System Design

Okay, let's zoom in on a particularly challenging aspect of software architecture: designing systems that can scale. Scalability is all about building applications that can handle increasing demands. Think about it: a website that works fine with 100 users might crash when it gets 10,000 users. We want to avoid that!

Designing for scalability is tough because it involves a lot of complex decisions and trade-offs.

We need to think about:

- Choosing the right technologies: Should we use a relational database or a NoSQL database? Do we need a message queue? A caching system?
- Designing distributed systems: How do we break down our application into smaller, independent services that can run on multiple servers?
- Implementing load balancing: How do we distribute incoming traffic evenly across those servers?
- Monitoring and performance tuning: How do we track how our system is performing and make adjustments to optimize it?

It's a bit like designing a city's infrastructure. You need to plan for growth, traffic flow, resource allocation, and so on.

Generative AI has the potential to automate many of these decisions, making it much easier to build scalable systems. Let's see how.

1. Suggesting Scaling Strategies

AI models, trained on data about various system architectures and their performance under different loads, can analyze our application's requirements and suggest appropriate scaling strategies.

For example, if we tell the AI that our application is expected to experience a sudden surge in traffic during peak hours, it might suggest:

- Horizontal scaling: Adding more servers to handle the increased load.

- Caching: Storing frequently accessed data in memory to reduce database load.
- Message queues: Using asynchronous communication to decouple components and improve responsiveness.

Or, if we tell the AI that our application needs to store a large amount of data, it might suggest:

- Database sharding: Dividing the database into smaller, more manageable pieces.
- NoSQL databases: Using databases that are designed for handling large volumes of unstructured data.

2. Generating Configuration Code

Setting up scalable systems often involves writing a lot of configuration code for different technologies. This can be tedious and error-prone. AI can automate this process by generating the configuration code for us.

For example, if we're using a load balancer like Nginx, the AI could generate the Nginx configuration file based on our application's requirements.

Here's a simplified example of how this might look. Let's say we have a Python function that uses the subprocess module to interact with Nginx.

```
Python

import subprocess


def generate_nginx_config(upstream_servers,
listen_port):

    """ """ """
```

Generates an Nginx configuration for load balancing.

Args:

upstream_servers (list): A list of server addresses (e.g., ["192.168.1.10:8000", "192.168.1.11:8000"]).

listen_port (int): The port Nginx should listen on.

Returns:

str: The Nginx configuration.

"""


```
upstream_block = "upstream my_backend {\n"

for server in upstream_servers:

    upstream_block += f"    server {server};\n"

upstream_block += "}\n\n"


server_block = f"server {{\n    listen {listen_port};\n\n    location / {{\n    proxy_pass http://my_backend;\n    proxy_set_header Host $host;\n
```

```
proxy_set_header X-Real-IP $remote_addr;\n
proxy_set_header X-Forwarded-For
$proxy_add_x_forwarded_for;\n
proxy_set_header X-Forwarded-Proto $scheme;\n
}}\n}}"


    return upstream_block + server_block



# Example Usage (replace with your actual server
addresses and port)

servers = ["192.168.1.10:8000",
"192.168.1.11:8000"]

port = 80

nginx_config = generate_nginx_config(servers,
port)



# Write the configuration to a file

with open("nginx.conf", "w") as f:

    f.write(nginx_config)



# Reload Nginx to apply the changes

subprocess.run(["sudo", "nginx", "-s", "reload"])
```

In a real-world scenario, you could provide the AI with information about your application's requirements (e.g., number of servers, traffic patterns, etc.), and it could generate a more sophisticated Nginx configuration.

3. Automating Deployment and Orchestration

Deploying and managing scalable systems can also be complex, often involving tools like Docker and Kubernetes. AI can automate some of the deployment and orchestration tasks.

For example, AI could:

- Generate Dockerfiles for different services.
- Create Kubernetes deployment and service configurations.
- Automate the scaling of services based on traffic.

This can significantly simplify the process of deploying and managing complex distributed systems.

It's important to remember that while AI can automate many aspects of scalable system design, human expertise is still crucial.

We need to:

- Review the AI's suggestions: Ensure that the generated configurations and deployments are correct and appropriate for our specific needs.
- Understand the trade-offs: Scalability often involves trade-offs between cost, performance, and complexity. We need to make informed decisions about these trade-offs.
- Monitor the system closely: Even with AI assistance, we need to monitor the system's performance and make adjustments as needed.

Automating scalable system design with AI has the potential to significantly improve our productivity and allow us to build more robust and efficient applications. It's an exciting area where AI can really make a difference.

9.3 Future of AI-Driven Architecture

Alright, let's look ahead. We've talked about how AI is starting to assist with software architecture, but what does the future hold? It's a field that's evolving rapidly, and I think we're on the cusp of some pretty significant changes.

The potential for AI to influence how we design and build software is enormous. It's not just about automating a few tasks; it's about fundamentally shifting the software development lifecycle.

Here's how I see things progressing:

1. Automated Architectural Decisions

Right now, AI can provide suggestions and assistance. But in the future, we might see AI systems that can automatically make architectural decisions.

Think about it: AI models could analyze a project's requirements, constraints, and even the development team's capabilities, and then automatically select the most suitable architectural patterns, technologies, and deployment strategies.

For example, you could give an AI system a high-level description of an application, like:

"Build a real-time collaboration tool for editing documents. It needs to support multiple users editing simultaneously, with low latency and strong consistency. It should also be scalable to handle a large number of users."

The AI could then automatically decide on:

- A suitable data synchronization strategy (e.g., Operational Transformation or Conflict-free Replicated Data Types).
- The appropriate communication protocols (e.g., WebSockets).

- The optimal database architecture (e.g., a distributed database).
- The best deployment model (e.g., cloud-based serverless functions).

This level of automation could significantly speed up the initial development process and reduce the need for manual architectural design.

2. Code Generation from Architectural Models

Currently, AI might generate code snippets or basic structures. But in the future, AI could potentially generate a large portion of the application's code directly from architectural models.

You could design the architecture using a visual tool or a specialized language, and the AI would then translate that design into executable code.

For example, you could use a tool to create a diagram showing the different services in a microservices architecture, their dependencies, and their communication patterns. The AI would then generate the code for each service, including:

- API endpoints
- Data access logic
- Business logic
- Communication handling

This could drastically reduce the amount of manual coding required, allowing developers to focus on higher-level tasks and complex business logic.

3. Continuous Architectural Optimization

Software systems are not static; they evolve over time. New features are added, traffic patterns change, and technology advances. AI could play a role in continuously optimizing the architecture of a running system.

AI systems could:

- Monitor system performance: Track metrics like latency, throughput, and resource utilization.
- Analyze system behavior: Identify bottlenecks, inefficiencies, and potential problems.
- Suggest architectural changes: Recommend changes to the architecture to improve performance, scalability, or reliability.
- Automate architectural adjustments: In some cases, AI might even be able to automatically adjust the system's architecture, such as scaling up or down resources, or rerouting traffic.

This would create a self-optimizing system that adapts to changing conditions and maintains optimal performance.

The Potential Impact

The widespread adoption of AI-driven architecture could have a profound impact on software development:

- Faster Development Cycles: Applications could be built much more quickly, reducing time to market.
- Improved Software Quality: Systems could be more robust, scalable, and secure due to AI's ability to analyze and optimize designs.
- Reduced Development Costs: The cost of building and maintaining software could be significantly reduced, as AI automates many tasks.
- Democratization of Software Development: AI tools could make software development more accessible to a wider range of people, even those without extensive programming experience.

Ethical Considerations

However, it's crucial to acknowledge that AI-driven architecture also raises important ethical considerations:

- Job Displacement: The automation of architectural tasks could lead to job displacement for some software developers.
- Bias and Fairness: AI models could perpetuate biases present in the data they're trained on, leading to unfair or discriminatory architectural decisions.
- Lack of Explainability: It might be difficult to understand why an AI system has made a particular architectural decision, which could erode trust.
- Security Risks: AI-generated architectures might contain unforeseen security vulnerabilities.

To navigate these challenges, we need to:

- Focus on Human-AI Collaboration: Encourage a collaborative approach where AI assists human architects, rather than replacing them entirely.
- Develop Ethical AI Principles: Establish clear ethical guidelines for the development and use of AI in software architecture.
- Promote Transparency and Explainability: Design AI systems that can explain their reasoning and decision-making processes.
- Prioritize Security: Ensure that AI-generated architectures are thoroughly vetted for security vulnerabilities.

The future of software architecture is likely to be a blend of human creativity and AI automation. AI can handle the complexities and repetitive tasks, while human architects can provide the crucial oversight, ethical guidance, and innovative thinking that are still essential for building truly great software systems.

Chapter 10: The Future of AI-Assisted Coding

This chapter explores the emerging trends in generative AI and their potential impact on the future of coding. We'll discuss the evolving role of AI in software development and how developers can prepare for an AI-driven future.

10.1 Emerging Trends in Generative AI

Okay, let's talk about where generative AI is headed, especially in the context of coding. This field is moving incredibly fast, and it's important to stay ahead of the curve. It's not just about what AI can do *now*; it's about what it will be able to do in the very near future.

The landscape of generative AI is dynamic, with new breakthroughs and applications appearing regularly.

Here are some of the key trends that I think are going to significantly shape how we code:

1. Increased Model Capabilities

AI models are simply getting better, and it's not just a small improvement.

We're seeing exponential growth in their ability to handle complex tasks:

- Larger Models, More Power: Models are being trained with more parameters and on larger datasets. This allows them to capture more nuanced relationships in code and generate more sophisticated and comprehensive code.
- Handling More Languages and Paradigms: Early code generation models might have been good at Python or

JavaScript. Newer models are becoming proficient in a wider range of languages, including less common or domain-specific languages. They're also starting to understand different programming paradigms, like object-oriented, functional, and concurrent programming.

- Beyond Code Snippets: Initially, AI might have been good at generating small code snippets. Now, they can generate entire functions, classes, modules, and even complete applications. This is a game-changer for speeding up development.

To illustrate this, consider the evolution of how AI might handle a complex code generation task:

- Early Stage: You might give an AI a prompt like: "Write a function to sort a list of integers in Python." The AI generates the basic sorting logic.
- Current Stage: You give a prompt like: "Write a Python class that implements a binary search tree data structure, including methods for insertion, search, and deletion." The AI generates a more complete class definition, including methods and basic error handling.
- Future Stage: You give a prompt like: "Generate a web application using Django that allows users to create, view, edit, and delete blog posts, with user authentication and authorization." The AI generates a significant portion of the application's code, including models, views, URLs, and basic templates.

2. Improved Contextual Understanding

One of the key challenges for AI in code generation is understanding the context of the code. Code isn't written in isolation; it's part of a larger project with its own architecture, conventions, and dependencies.

AI models are getting much better at this:

- Project-Level Awareness: AI is starting to understand the overall structure of a project, including how different modules and components are connected. This allows it to generate code that fits seamlessly into the existing codebase.
- Coding Style Recognition: AI can learn the coding style of a team or project and generate code that adheres to those conventions. This improves consistency and readability.
- Dependency Management: AI can understand the dependencies between different parts of the code and suggest appropriate libraries and frameworks to use.

For example, if you're working on a project that heavily uses a specific library, the AI will be more likely to use that library in the generated code. It will also be able to generate code that interacts correctly with the existing code in the project.

3. Multimodal AI

This is a really exciting area. AI models are starting to combine different types of information, not just text and code.

This "multimodal" approach opens up new possibilities:

- Code from Diagrams: You could draw a UML diagram and the AI generates the corresponding code.
- Code from Mockups: You could provide a visual mockup of a user interface, and the AI generates the HTML, CSS, and JavaScript.
- Code from Natural Language Descriptions: You could describe a complex algorithm or system functionality in plain English, and the AI translates it into code.

Here's a conceptual example:

You provide the AI with a simple diagram:

[User Interface] --> (API) --> [Database]

And a natural language description:

"The API should allow users to create, retrieve, update, and delete products. Product data includes name, description, and price."

The AI could then generate the code for the API endpoints, the database schema, and even basic user interface elements.

4. AI-Driven Code Refinement

AI is increasingly capable of not just generating code but also improving existing code:

- Automated Bug Fixing: AI can analyze code and automatically identify and fix common types of errors, such as syntax errors, logical errors, and security vulnerabilities.
- Performance Optimization: AI can suggest ways to make code run faster and more efficiently, such as using more efficient algorithms or data structures.
- Security Hardening: AI can identify potential security risks in code and suggest ways to mitigate them, such as preventing SQL injection or cross-site scripting attacks.

5. Integration into Development Environments

AI tools are becoming more tightly integrated into IDEs (Integrated Development Environments) and other coding tools.

This makes it easier for developers to access and use AI assistance:

- AI-Powered Autocomplete: Think of autocomplete on steroids. AI can suggest entire blocks of code, not just single words or lines.

- Context-Aware Suggestions: AI can provide suggestions that are tailored to the specific context of the code you're writing.
- Real-time Code Analysis: AI can analyze your code as you write it and provide immediate feedback and suggestions.

6. Democratization of Software Development

Perhaps the most significant long-term trend is that AI is making coding more accessible to a wider range of people.

- Beginner-Friendly Tools: AI can help beginners learn to code, understand complex concepts, and build applications more easily.
- Low-Code/No-Code Platforms: AI is powering the development of low-code and no-code platforms, which allow people to build applications without writing code.
- Domain Expert Development: AI is enabling domain experts (e.g., scientists, artists, business analysts) to create software tailored to their needs, even if they don't have extensive programming skills.

These trends are transforming the landscape of software development. It's an exciting time to be a coder, and the possibilities are truly vast.

10.2 Impact on the Future of Coding

Okay, so we've looked at the emerging trends. Now, let's really think about how all this AI stuff is going to change what it means to be a coder. It's not just about some new tools; it's about a fundamental shift in how we approach software development.

Here's how I see the impact unfolding:

1. Shift in Developer Focus

I think one of the biggest changes is going to be a shift in what developers spend their time on. We'll likely move away from writing a lot of the repetitive, boilerplate code and towards more high-level, creative, and problem-solving tasks.

- Less Code, More Design: AI can handle a lot of the code generation, so developers will spend more time designing the overall architecture of systems, defining the requirements, and ensuring that everything fits together. This is where those "big picture" skills become even more valuable.
- Emphasis on Problem-Solving: AI can help implement solutions, but it's up to us to define the *problems* in the first place. We'll need to be really good at analyzing complex situations, breaking them down into manageable parts, and figuring out the best approach.
- Increased Innovation: With AI handling the more tedious parts of coding, developers will have more time and mental energy to focus on innovation. This could lead to the creation of entirely new types of software and applications.

Think of it like this: instead of spending hours writing the code for a user interface, you might spend that time designing a more intuitive and user-friendly experience. Instead of debugging a complex algorithm, you might spend that time figuring out the best way to solve a business problem with software.

2. Increased Productivity

This one's pretty straightforward. AI tools will help developers write code much faster and more efficiently.

- Speeding Up Development: AI can generate code snippets, complete functions, and even create entire modules in a fraction of the time it would take a human developer. This will significantly speed up the development process.

- Reducing Errors: AI can help catch common coding errors, such as syntax errors, type errors, and logic errors, before they cause problems. This will lead to more robust and reliable software.
- Automation of Repetitive Tasks: AI can automate many repetitive tasks, such as generating boilerplate code, writing unit tests, and refactoring code. This will free up developers to focus on more important work.

It's like having a super-powered assistant that can handle a lot of the grunt work, allowing you to focus on the more creative and strategic aspects of your job.

3. New Development Workflows

AI will also change how we develop software. It's not just about using AI to write code; it's about integrating AI into our entire workflow.

- AI-Assisted Design: AI could help us design software architectures, user interfaces, and even database schemas.
- AI-Driven Development: AI could guide us through the development process, suggesting the best way to implement a feature or solve a problem.
- AI-Powered Testing: AI could automate the creation and execution of tests, ensuring that our code is robust and reliable.
- Continuous AI Feedback: AI could provide continuous feedback on our code as we write it, suggesting improvements and catching potential errors.

This will lead to more collaborative and iterative development processes, with AI acting as a partner to human developers.

4. Emphasis on Prompt Engineering

If AI is going to generate a lot of our code, then the skill of writing effective prompts will become incredibly important.

- Clarity and Precision: We'll need to be very precise in our instructions to the AI, clearly specifying what we want it to do.
- Context and Constraints: We'll need to provide the AI with enough context about the project, the requirements, and any constraints.
- Prompt Design: We might even see the emergence of "prompt engineers," developers who specialize in crafting effective prompts for AI code generation.

It's a bit like learning to communicate with a very intelligent but also very literal being. You need to be clear, concise, and unambiguous.

5. Importance of Code Review

Even with AI, code review will remain crucial, and it might even become more important.

- Ensuring Correctness: We'll need to carefully review AI-generated code to ensure that it's correct and does what we intend.
- Maintaining Quality: We'll need to make sure that the AI-generated code meets our coding standards and is maintainable.
- Ethical Considerations: We'll need to be vigilant about potential biases or security vulnerabilities in AI-generated code.

Code review will become a critical safeguard to ensure that AI is a helpful tool, not a source of problems.

6. Augmented Creativity

Finally, and perhaps most excitingly, AI can augment our creativity as developers.

- Exploring New Ideas: AI can help us generate and explore different design options, code structures, and solutions.
- Breaking Creative Blocks: AI can help us overcome creative blocks by providing fresh perspectives and suggesting novel approaches.
- Expanding the Scope of Possibilities: AI can help us build more complex and ambitious software projects than we could before.

AI can be a partner in the creative process, helping us push the boundaries of what's possible with software.

In short, the future of coding is going to be incredibly dynamic and exciting. AI is changing the game, and we as developers need to adapt and evolve to thrive in this new landscape. It's about embracing AI as a powerful tool and focusing on the uniquely human skills that will always be essential in software development.

10.3 Preparing for AI-Driven Development

Okay, so we've talked a lot about the changes AI is bringing to the world of coding. The big question now is: how do we, as developers, get ready for this new era? It's not about fearing the change; it's about embracing it and equipping ourselves with the skills and mindset to thrive.

Let's break down some key strategies:

1. Embrace Continuous Learning

This is paramount. The field of AI is evolving at a breakneck pace. What's cutting-edge today might be commonplace tomorrow. We need to be lifelong learners, constantly updating our knowledge and skills.

- Stay Updated: Follow industry news, read research papers, attend conferences, and participate in online communities. Keep an eye on the latest advancements in generative AI, language models, and related technologies.
- Explore New Tools and Technologies: Don't be afraid to experiment with new AI-powered coding tools and libraries. Try out different code generation models, prompt engineering platforms, and AI-assisted debugging tools.
- Develop a Growth Mindset: Cultivate a mindset that embraces change and views challenges as opportunities for growth. Be willing to step outside your comfort zone and learn new things.

It's like keeping your tools sharp. You wouldn't use the same rusty old hammer for every job, right? You need to acquire and master the latest tools in the AI-driven coding workshop.

2. Develop Strong Problem-Solving Skills

AI can help us implement solutions, but it's still up to us to define the problems and design the solutions. This requires strong problem-solving skills, which will become even more valuable in the age of AI.

- Analytical Thinking: Sharpen your ability to analyze complex problems, break them down into smaller, more manageable parts, and identify the root causes.
- Critical Thinking: Develop your ability to evaluate information, identify assumptions, and make sound judgments.
- Design Thinking: Learn to approach problems with a user-centered perspective, focusing on understanding user needs and creating innovative solutions.

- Systems Thinking: Cultivate the ability to see how different parts of a system interact and understand the broader context of a problem.

Think of it like being a detective. AI can help you gather evidence, but you need to be able to analyze the evidence, identify the suspects, and solve the case.

3. Master Prompt Engineering

As AI becomes more involved in code generation, the skill of writing effective prompts will become increasingly important. We'll need to learn how to communicate our intentions clearly and precisely to the AI.

- Clarity and Precision: Practice writing clear and concise prompts that specify the desired functionality, inputs, outputs, and constraints.
- Context and Detail: Learn to provide the AI with enough context about the project, the requirements, and any relevant details.
- Prompt Design Patterns: Explore different prompt design patterns and techniques, such as few-shot learning, chain-of-thought prompting, and role prompting.
- Iterative Refinement: Develop the ability to refine your prompts iteratively based on the AI's output, gradually improving the quality of the generated code.

It's like learning to speak a new language, the language of AI. You need to learn the grammar, the vocabulary, and the nuances of communication to get the best results.

4. Enhance Code Review Skills

Even with AI assistance, code review will remain crucial, and it might even become more critical. We'll need to be able to critically evaluate AI-generated code to ensure its quality, correctness, and security.

- Code Quality: Develop a strong understanding of coding standards, best practices, and design principles.
- Error Detection: Improve your ability to identify potential errors, bugs, and logical flaws in code.
- Security Awareness: Learn to recognize common security vulnerabilities, such as SQL injection and cross-site scripting.
- Testing Strategies: Master different testing techniques to ensure the code is robust and reliable.

Think of it as being a quality control expert. You need to be able to spot any defects in the AI-generated code and ensure that it meets the highest standards.

5. Cultivate Collaboration Skills

The future of software development will likely involve a close collaboration between human developers and AI tools. We need to learn how to work effectively in this new collaborative environment.

- AI as a Partner: View AI as a helpful assistant, not as a replacement for human developers.
- Shared Responsibility: Understand that the responsibility for the quality and correctness of the code is shared between the developer and the AI.
- Effective Communication: Learn to communicate effectively with AI tools, providing clear instructions and feedback.
- Teamwork: Continue to develop your ability to collaborate with other developers, sharing knowledge and expertise.

It's like learning to work in a team with a new, very efficient but also very literal team member. You need to learn how to communicate effectively and leverage each other's strengths.

6. Focus on Creativity and Innovation

AI can automate many routine coding tasks, freeing up developers to focus on more creative and innovative work. We need to cultivate our ability to think creatively and come up with new and exciting software solutions.

- Design Thinking: Learn to apply design thinking principles to create user-centered and innovative software.
- Brainstorming and Ideation: Practice brainstorming techniques to generate new ideas and explore different possibilities.
- Experimentation: Be willing to experiment with new technologies and approaches, and don't be afraid to fail.
- Continuous Improvement: Strive to continuously improve your creative process and explore new ways to innovate.

Think of it as being an artist. AI can provide you with the tools and materials, but you need to bring your own creativity and vision to create something truly unique and impactful.

7. Ethics and Responsibility

Finally, and perhaps most importantly, we need to develop a strong understanding of the ethical implications of AI and use these tools responsibly.

- Bias Awareness: Be aware of the potential for bias in AI-generated code and take steps to mitigate it.
- Security and Privacy: Prioritize security and privacy in your software development practices.
- Transparency and Explainability: Strive to create AI systems that are transparent and explainable.
- Social Impact: Consider the broader social impact of your work and use AI to create positive change.

It's like being a responsible citizen. You need to be aware of the consequences of your actions and use your skills to make the world a better place.

By embracing these strategies, we can prepare ourselves for the AI-driven future of coding and become more effective, creative, and responsible developers.

Chapter 11: Ethical Considerations and Responsible AI

This chapter explores the ethical challenges raised by generative AI in software development and provides guidelines for responsible use. We'll discuss bias and fairness, security implications, intellectual property issues, and best practices for developing AI-powered tools.

11.1 Bias and Fairness in AI-Generated Code

Alright, let's have a really important discussion – bias and fairness in AI-generated code. This isn't just a theoretical concern; it has real-world implications that we need to address head-on as developers.

The crux of the issue is that AI models learn from the data they're trained on. If that training data contains biases – and let's face it, much of the data we have *does* reflect existing societal biases – then the AI model will likely learn those biases and perpetuate them in the code it generates.

Think about it this way: AI models are like students. They learn from the examples you give them. If you only show them examples of one type of code or code written by a certain demographic, they'll naturally start to favor that type of code.

Here's how this can manifest in AI-generated code:

- Stereotypical Code Generation: The AI might generate code that makes assumptions about who is likely to use certain software or perform certain roles. For example, it might generate code that assumes that all users are male or that all system administrators are male.

- Unequal Treatment: AI-generated systems that make decisions based on code can unfairly disadvantage certain groups. This is particularly concerning in areas like:
    - Hiring systems: AI might generate code that filters out candidates based on gender, race, or other protected characteristics.
    - Loan application systems: AI might generate code that denies loans to certain groups based on biased historical data.
    - Criminal justice systems: AI might generate code that predicts recidivism (the likelihood of reoffending) in a way that disproportionately targets certain communities.
- Lack of Representation: AI might generate code that doesn't adequately address the needs or perspectives of diverse users. For example, it might generate code that only supports a limited set of languages or that doesn't consider the needs of users with disabilities.

To really grasp the potential for bias, let's consider some more detailed examples:

1. Bias in Code Comments and Documentation

AI models trained on code often learn to generate comments and documentation. If the training data contains comments with biased language, the AI might reproduce that bias.

For instance, consider a simplified scenario where the training data contains comments that frequently use gendered pronouns when referring to developers:

Python

```
# Original code comment (from training
data):
```

```
# The engineer should check if he has write
access.
```

An AI model trained on such data might generate code with comments like this:

Python

```python
def process_data(data):

    # The programmer should ensure he
handles null values.

    # ... code ...
```

This perpetuates the stereotype that all programmers are male.

2. Bias in Feature Selection

AI models can also be used to generate code that selects features for machine learning models. If the training data for the feature selection model is biased, the generated code can also be biased.

For example, suppose you're building a loan application system. The training data contains historical loan data, and it happens to show that historically, women have had slightly higher default rates than men. An AI model trained on this data might generate code that includes gender as a feature in the loan application system. This could lead to women being unfairly disadvantaged, even if the historical difference is due to other factors (e.g., societal inequalities).

Python

```python
# Simplified example (illustrative):
```

```
def select_loan_features(applicant_data):

    features = ['age', 'income',
'credit_score']

    if applicant_data['gender'] == 'female':
# Potentially biased feature selection


features.append('employment_history')

    return features
```

This code snippet, generated by a biased AI, adds employment_history as a feature *only* for female applicants, which is discriminatory.

3. Bias in Algorithm Implementation

Even if the input data and feature selection are unbiased, AI can introduce bias in how it implements algorithms.

Consider generating code for a search algorithm. If the training data contains examples where certain results are consistently ranked higher for specific groups, the AI might generate code that replicates this ranking bias.

```
Python

# Simplified example (illustrative):

def search_results(query, user_group):

    results = perform_search(query)

    if user_group == 'group_a':
```

```
        results.sort(key=lambda x:
x['relevance'] + x['group_a_boost']) #
Biased ranking

    else:

        results.sort(key=lambda x:
x['relevance'])

    return results
```

This code snippet, generated by a biased AI, adds a group_a_boost to the relevance score for users in 'group_a', unfairly favoring those results.

Addressing Bias: A Multi-faceted Approach

Tackling bias in AI-generated code requires a comprehensive strategy:

- Data Curation: The most crucial step is to carefully curate the training data.
  - Representation: Ensure that your datasets are representative of the diversity of the population.
  - Balance: Make sure that different groups are equally represented in the data.
  - Cleaning: Remove or mitigate any existing biases in the data. This might involve removing biased language, correcting skewed distributions, or using data augmentation techniques.
- Bias Evaluation: Develop methods to assess AI models and their generated code for bias.
  - Metrics: Define metrics to measure fairness, such as equal opportunity, demographic parity, and equalized odds.

- ○ Analysis: Analyze the model's output for patterns that indicate bias.
- ○ Auditing: Conduct regular audits of AI systems to ensure they are fair and unbiased.
- Fairness-Aware Techniques: Implement algorithms and methods that are specifically designed to promote fairness in AI.
  - ○ Pre-processing: Modify the training data to remove bias before training the model.
  - ○ In-processing: Modify the model's training process to encourage fairness.
  - ○ Post-processing: Modify the model's output to remove bias after it has been generated.
- Transparency and Explainability: Design AI systems that are transparent and explainable. This can help us understand why the model is generating certain code and identify potential sources of bias.
- Ethical Guidelines: Establish clear ethical guidelines for the development and use of AI in code generation. These guidelines should emphasize fairness, accountability, and transparency.

Bias in AI-generated code is a complex challenge, but it's one that we must address proactively. By understanding the sources of bias and implementing effective mitigation strategies, we can ensure that AI is used to create code that is fair, equitable, and beneficial to all.

11.2 Security Implications

Okay, let's have a straight talk about security. When we're dealing with AI-generated code, it's not just about whether the code works; it's about whether it's *safe*.[1] AI can be a powerful tool, but it can also introduce new security risks if we're not careful.[2]

The problem is that AI models learn from the code they're trained on. If that training data contains code with security vulnerabilities, the AI might inadvertently reproduce those vulnerabilities in the code it generates.[3] It's like a student learning bad habits from a teacher.

Here are some of the key security implications we need to be aware of:

1. Vulnerable Code Patterns

AI models might generate code that uses insecure coding practices.[4]

This can lead to various vulnerabilities, such as:

SQL Injection: This occurs when user input is directly inserted into a SQL query without proper sanitization.[5] Attackers can then inject malicious SQL code to manipulate the database.[6]

For example, consider this (simplified) PHP code:

PHP

```php
$username = $_GET['username'];

$query = "SELECT * FROM users WHERE username = '$username'";

// ... execute query ...
```

An AI model might generate this code because it's a common pattern, but it's highly vulnerable to SQL injection. If a user enters a malicious string as their username (e.g., ' OR '1'='1), it can alter the query and potentially expose sensitive data.

Cross-Site Scripting (XSS): This occurs when user input is displayed on a web page without proper escaping. Attackers can then inject malicious JavaScript code into the page, which can steal user cookies or perform other harmful actions.[7]

For example, consider this (simplified) JavaScript code:

JavaScript

```
function displayUserName(username) {

    document.getElementById('user-greeting').inn
    erHTML = "Hello, " + username;

}
```

If the username variable contains malicious JavaScript code, it will be executed when the page is displayed.

Buffer Overflows: These occur when a program writes more data to a buffer than it can hold, potentially overwriting adjacent memory and causing crashes[8] or security breaches.[9] AI might generate code that doesn't properly handle buffer sizes, leading to this vulnerability.[10]

Insecure Deserialization: This occurs when untrusted data is deserialized (converted from a serialized format back into an object) without proper validation.[11] Attackers can manipulate the serialized data to execute arbitrary code.[12] AI might generate code that uses insecure deserialization techniques.[13]

2. Dependence on Insecure Libraries

AI models might suggest or use libraries that are known to have security flaws.[14] This can introduce vulnerabilities into the generated code.

For example, if an AI model is trained on a dataset that includes code using an outdated version of a library with a known security vulnerability, it might generate code that uses that same vulnerable version.[15]

3. Lack of Robust Error Handling

AI models might generate code that doesn't handle errors properly. This can create opportunities for attackers to exploit unexpected behavior.

For example, if an AI model generates code that doesn't validate user input, it might be vulnerable to injection attacks.[16] Or, if it generates code that doesn't handle exceptions gracefully, it might crash or expose sensitive information when an error occurs.

4. AI as an Attack Surface

In some cases, the AI model itself might become an attack surface. If an attacker can manipulate the input to the AI model, they might be able to influence the generated code in a malicious way.[17]

For example, if you have an AI-powered code generation tool that's accessible via an API, an attacker might try to craft specific prompts that cause the AI to generate code with vulnerabilities.

How to Mitigate Security Risks

To address these security concerns, we need a multi-layered approach:

- Train on Secure Code: The most fundamental step is to train AI models on datasets that emphasize secure coding practices. This includes:
  - Secure Coding Guidelines: Include examples of code that follows well-established security guidelines (e.g., OWASP guidelines).
  - Vulnerability-Free Code: Train on code from projects that have undergone rigorous security audits and have a low vulnerability rate.
  - Negative Examples: Include examples of code with known vulnerabilities, along with annotations explaining the risks.
- Implement Security Analysis Tools: Develop AI-powered tools that can automatically analyze AI-generated code for security vulnerabilities. These tools could:
  - Static Analysis: Analyze the code without executing it to identify potential vulnerabilities.[18]
  - Dynamic Analysis: Analyze the code's behavior during execution to detect security flaws.[19]
  - Fuzzing: Automatically generate test inputs to try to trigger vulnerabilities in the code.
- Educate Developers: It's crucial to train developers on how to identify and prevent security risks in AI-generated code. This includes:
  - Security Best Practices: Emphasize the importance of secure coding principles.[20]
  - AI Limitations: Make developers aware of the potential limitations of AI in generating secure code.[21]

- o Code Review: Stress the importance of thorough code review, especially when dealing with AI-generated code.
- Robust Testing: Implement comprehensive testing strategies, including security testing, to validate the generated code.
- Secure API Design: If using AI code generation via APIs, ensure the API itself is secure and resistant to attacks.

Security is paramount, and it's a shared responsibility. We need to be proactive in identifying and mitigating the security risks associated with AI-generated code. By combining AI's analytical capabilities with our human expertise and vigilance, we can build more secure and reliable software.

11.3 Intellectual Property and Ownership

Okay, this is where things get a bit complex and even legally murky: intellectual property (IP) and ownership when it comes to AI-generated code. It's a topic that's currently being debated, and there are no easy, universally agreed-upon answers.

The core of the issue is this: AI models are trained on existing code, which is often subject to copyright. So, when an AI generates new code, questions arise about who owns that code and whether it infringes on existing copyrights.

Let's break down the key areas of concern:

1. Training Data Ownership

AI models learn by analyzing massive amounts of code. This training data often includes code from open-source projects, commercial software, and various online repositories. Many of these sources are protected by copyright.

The question is: does training an AI model on copyrighted code constitute copyright infringement?

- Some argue that it's similar to a human learning from reading books. The AI learns patterns and structures, but it doesn't necessarily copy the original code verbatim. This view often leans on the concept of "fair use" or similar exceptions in copyright law.
- Others argue that training on copyrighted code creates a derivative work, and permission from the copyright holders is required.

There's no definitive legal consensus on this yet. Courts around the world are starting to grapple with these questions, and the legal landscape is still evolving.

2. AI as an Author

Another complex issue is whether an AI model can be considered an "author" of the code it generates. Copyright law typically grants ownership to human authors.

- If an AI generates code with minimal human intervention, can the AI be considered the author? If so, who owns the copyright? The AI's creator? The user who prompted the AI?
- If a human developer significantly modifies and improves AI-generated code, the human developer is clearly the author of those modifications. But what about the original AI-generated portion?

Again, current copyright law isn't well-equipped to handle these scenarios. Some legal scholars propose new frameworks for AI-generated works, while others try to apply existing copyright principles (often with difficulty).

3. Liability

Who is liable if AI-generated code causes harm or damage?

- If the code contains a security vulnerability that leads to a data breach, who is responsible? The AI's creator? The user who used the AI?
- If the code malfunctions and causes financial losses, who is held accountable?

Liability is a crucial issue, especially in safety-critical applications.

Illustrative Examples and Challenges

To make these issues more concrete, let's consider some examples:

- Open-Source Code: Much of the code used to train AI models comes from open-source projects. These projects often have permissive licenses (like MIT or Apache), which allow for commercial use and modification. However, even with permissive licenses, there can be questions about attribution and modification requirements.
- Commercial Code: If an AI model is trained on a dataset that includes copyrighted commercial code, the legal risks are higher. Using AI to generate code that closely resembles that commercial code could be considered infringement.
- AI-Generated Art: The debate about AI authorship is similar to the one surrounding AI-generated art. Some argue that AI is just a tool, and the human user is the true artist. Others argue that AI has a degree of creativity and autonomy, and it should be recognized as an author (or at least a co-author).
- Derivative Works: If an AI model generates code that is heavily based on existing code, the generated code might be considered a derivative work. This means that the original

copyright holder might have some claim to the generated code.

Practical Implications for Developers

So, what does all this mean for you as a developer using AI code generation tools?

Here are some key takeaways:

- Be Aware of the Legal Uncertainty: The legal landscape around AI-generated code is still evolving. There are no definitive answers to many of the questions surrounding ownership and copyright.
- Use Publicly Available Datasets: When possible, try to use AI models trained on publicly available datasets with clear and permissive licenses. This can help reduce the risk of copyright infringement.
- Document Your Usage: Keep detailed records of how you used AI to generate code, including the prompts you used and the modifications you made. This can be helpful in establishing your own authorship.
- Seek Legal Counsel: If you have significant concerns about the legal implications of using AI-generated code, consult with a lawyer specializing in intellectual property law.
- Follow Best Practices: Adhere to good coding practices, including proper attribution of any code you use from other sources (even if it's AI-generated).

The intersection of AI and intellectual property is a complex and rapidly changing area. We, as developers, need to stay informed, act responsibly, and contribute to the ongoing discussions about how to navigate these challenges ethically and legally.

11.4 Guidelines for Responsible Use

Okay, we've talked about the exciting potential of AI in coding, but we've also tackled the serious ethical and legal questions it raises. Now, let's put it all together and discuss some concrete guidelines for using AI code generation tools in a responsible and ethical way. It's about building a future where AI empowers us, not one where it creates new problems.

Think of these guidelines as a code of conduct for AI-assisted development. They're not just suggestions; they're principles to help us navigate this evolving landscape.

1. Prioritize Human Oversight

This is the golden rule: never treat AI-generated code as a black box that you can blindly trust. Always remember that you, as the developer, are ultimately responsible.

Code Review is Crucial: Treat AI-generated code with the same level of scrutiny (or even more) as code written by a junior developer.

Conduct thorough code reviews to check for:

- Correctness: Does the code actually do what it's supposed to do?
- Efficiency: Is the code well-optimized and performant?
- Security: Does the code contain any security vulnerabilities?
- Readability: Is the code clear, concise, and easy to understand?
- Style: Does the code adhere to your project's coding standards?

Testing is Essential: Don't rely solely on visual inspection. Write comprehensive unit tests, integration tests, and end-to-end tests to verify the code's behavior in different scenarios. Pay extra attention to edge cases and error handling.

Maintain Control: Use AI as a tool to assist you, not to replace your judgment. You should always have the final say in what code is included in your project.

2. Be Aware of Limitations

AI models are powerful, but they're not perfect.

They have limitations that we need to be aware of:

- Hallucinations: AI can sometimes generate code that looks correct but is actually wrong. It might generate code that compiles and runs but produces incorrect results or has unexpected side effects.
- Bias: As we discussed earlier, AI models can perpetuate and amplify biases present in their training data. This can lead to code that is unfair or discriminatory.
- Security Vulnerabilities: AI models might generate code that contains security vulnerabilities, such as SQL injection or cross-site scripting.
- Lack of Context: AI models may not fully understand the context of your project or the specific business requirements. This can lead to code that is suboptimal or inappropriate.

Recognizing these limitations is the first step in mitigating them.

3. Promote Transparency

Be open and honest about how you are using AI in your development process. This builds trust and allows for better collaboration.

Document AI Usage: Clearly document which parts of your code were generated by AI and which parts were written by humans.

Explain AI's Role: If using AI to generate code for a specific feature, explain how the AI was used and what its limitations were.

Acknowledge AI Contributions: If AI has made significant contributions to the code, consider acknowledging its role in the development process (where appropriate and ethically sound).

Transparency is especially important when dealing with AI-powered tools that interact directly with users.

4. Focus on Ethical Development

Strive to develop AI tools and use AI-generated code in a way that is fair, safe, and beneficial to society.

Prioritize Fairness: Actively work to mitigate bias in AI-generated code and ensure that your software treats all users equitably.

Ensure Safety: Thoroughly test AI-generated code to prevent errors and ensure that it doesn't pose any risks to users.

Protect Privacy: Handle user data responsibly and ensure that AI-generated code doesn't violate user privacy.

Promote Accessibility: Design and develop software that is accessible to users with disabilities.

Consider Social Impact: Think about the broader social impact of your work and use AI to create positive change.

5. Engage in Dialogue

The ethical and legal implications of AI in coding are still being debated. It's important to participate in these discussions and contribute to the development of best practices.

Stay Informed: Keep up-to-date with the latest research and discussions on AI ethics.

Share Your Experiences: Share your experiences and insights with other developers and researchers.

Contribute to Standards: Participate in the development of standards and guidelines for responsible AI use.

Advocate for Responsible AI: Advocate for policies and regulations that promote the ethical development and deployment of AI.

A Practical Example: Security Audits

Let's illustrate these guidelines with a practical example. Suppose you're using an AI tool to generate code for a web application.

Prioritize Human Oversight: You wouldn't just deploy the AI-generated code directly. You would have experienced security engineers perform a thorough security audit of the code, looking for vulnerabilities like SQL injection, XSS, and authentication weaknesses.

Be Aware of Limitations: You'd know that the AI might not have caught all potential security flaws, so you'd use a combination of automated security scanning tools and manual code review.

Promote Transparency: You'd document that the initial code structure was generated by AI and clearly outline the steps taken to ensure its security.

Focus on Ethical Development: You'd ensure that the application handles user data responsibly and protects user privacy.

By following these guidelines, we can harness the power of AI in coding while minimizing the risks and ensuring that we're building a better, more ethical future for software development.

Conclusion

We've reached the end of our exploration into the exciting and transformative world of generative AI for software developers. Throughout this book, we've navigated the fundamental concepts, practical applications, and the evolving landscape of this powerful technology.

We began by establishing the groundwork, understanding the core principles of generative AI, and equipping ourselves with the necessary tools and environment to effectively utilize these models. We then transitioned into the practical realm, focusing on the techniques for crafting effective prompts to guide AI code generation, automating routine development tasks, and even leveraging AI to enhance code refactoring.

As we progressed, we expanded our scope, examining the potential of generative AI to enable the creation of next-generation applications, from AI-powered chatbots and assistants to the automated generation of domain-specific languages and APIs.

However, we didn't shy away from the complexities. We critically assessed the limitations of AI-generated code, emphasizing the crucial role of human oversight in ensuring code quality, correctness, and security. We also dedicated significant attention to the ethical considerations surrounding AI in software development, addressing the challenges of bias, fairness, security, and intellectual property.

Ultimately, this book has aimed to provide you with a balanced and comprehensive understanding of generative AI in the context of software development. It's not just about the "how," but also the "why" and the "what next."

The key takeaway is that generative AI is not poised to replace software developers. Instead, it presents us with an opportunity to augment our abilities, streamline our workflows, and focus on the more creative and strategic aspects of our craft. It's about working *with* AI to build better software, faster.

The future of software development will undoubtedly be shaped by AI. As you move forward, I encourage you to embrace continuous learning, cultivate strong problem-solving skills, and prioritize ethical development practices. By doing so, you can position yourself at the forefront of this technological revolution and contribute to a future where AI empowers developers to create innovative and impactful solutions.

The journey with generative AI is just beginning, and I hope this book has provided you with a solid foundation and the inspiration to explore its vast potential. Keep coding, keep learning, and keep building the future!